# A REVIEW OF THE NEXT GENERATION AIR TRANSPORTATION SYSTEM

Implications and Importance of
*System Architecture*

David E. Liddle and Lynette I. Millett, *Editors*

Committee to Review the Enterprise Architecture, Software Development Approach, and Safety and Human Factor Design of the Next Generation Air Transportation System

Computer Science and Telecommunications Board

Division on Engineering and Physical Sciences

NATIONAL RESEARCH COUNCIL
*OF THE NATIONAL ACADEMIES*

THE NATIONAL ACADEMIES PRESS
Washington, D.C.
www.nap.edu

THE NATIONAL ACADEMIES PRESS    500 Fifth Street, NW    Washington, DC 20001

NOTICE: The project that is the subject of this report was approved by the Governing Board of the National Research Council, whose members are drawn from the councils of the National Academy of Sciences, the National Academy of Engineering, and the Institute of Medicine. The members of the committee responsible for the report were chosen for their special competences and with regard for appropriate balance.

This project was supported by the Federal Aviation Administration under award number DTFAWA-12-A-80013. Any opinions, findings, conclusions, or recommendations expressed in this publication are those of the author(s) and do not necessarily reflect the view of the organizations or agencies that provided support for this project.

International Standard Book Number 13:   978-0-309-37178-0
International Standard Book Number 10:   0-309-37178-3

Additional copies of this report are available from:

The National Academies Press
500 Fifth Street, NW, Keck 360
Washington, DC 20001
(800) 624-6242
(202) 334-3313
http://www.nap.edu

Copyright 2015 by the National Academy of Sciences. All rights reserved.

Printed in the United States of America

# THE NATIONAL ACADEMIES
*Advisers to the Nation on Science, Engineering, and Medicine*

The **National Academy of Sciences** is a private, nonprofit, self-perpetuating society of distinguished scholars engaged in scientific and engineering research, dedicated to the furtherance of science and technology and to their use for the general welfare. Upon the authority of the charter granted to it by the Congress in 1863, the Academy has a mandate that requires it to advise the federal government on scientific and technical matters. Dr. Ralph J. Cicerone is president of the National Academy of Sciences.

The **National Academy of Engineering** was established in 1964, under the charter of the National Academy of Sciences, as a parallel organization of outstanding engineers. It is autonomous in its administration and in the selection of its members, sharing with the National Academy of Sciences the responsibility for advising the federal government. The National Academy of Engineering also sponsors engineering programs aimed at meeting national needs, encourages education and research, and recognizes the superior achievements of engineers. Dr. C. D. Mote, Jr., is president of the National Academy of Engineering.

The **Institute of Medicine** was established in 1970 by the National Academy of Sciences to secure the services of eminent members of appropriate professions in the examination of policy matters pertaining to the health of the public. The Institute acts under the responsibility given to the National Academy of Sciences by its congressional charter to be an adviser to the federal government and, upon its own initiative, to identify issues of medical care, research, and education. Dr. Victor J. Dzau is president of the Institute of Medicine.

The **National Research Council** was organized by the National Academy of Sciences in 1916 to associate the broad community of science and technology with the Academy's purposes of furthering knowledge and advising the federal government. Functioning in accordance with general policies determined by the Academy, the Council has become the principal operating agency of both the National Academy of Sciences and the National Academy of Engineering in providing services to the government, the public, and the scientific and engineering communities. The Council is administered jointly by both Academies and the Institute of Medicine. Dr. Ralph J. Cicerone and Dr. C. D. Mote, Jr., are chair and vice chair, respectively, of the National Research Council.

www.national-academies.org

**Other Reports of the Computer Science and Telecommunications Board**

Bulk Collection of Signals Intelligence: Technical Options, 2015

Future Directions for NSF Advanced Computing Infrastructure to Support U.S. Science and Engineering in 2017-2020: An Interim Report, 2014
At the Nexus of Cybersecurity and Public Policy: Some Basic Concepts and Issues, 2014
Emerging and Readily Available Technologies and National Security: A Framework for Addressing Ethical, Legal, and Societal Issues, 2014

Geotargeted Alerts and Warnings: Report of a Workshop on Current Knowledge and Research Gaps, 2013
Professionalizing the Nation's Cybersecurity Workforce? Criteria for Future Decision-Making, 2013
Public Response to Alerts and Warnings Using Social Media: Summary of a Workshop on Current Knowledge and Research Gaps, 2013

Continuing Innovation in Information Technology, 2012
Computing Research for Sustainability, 2012
The Safety Challenge and Promise of Automotive Electronics: Insights from Unintended Acceleration, 2012 (with the Board on Energy and Environmental Systems and the Transportation Research Board)

Strategies and Priorities for Information Technology at the Centers for Medicare and Medicaid Services, 2011
The Future of Computing Performance: Game Over or Next Level?, 2011
Wireless Technology Prospects and Policy Options, 2011
Public Response to Alerts and Warnings on Mobile Devices: Summary of a Workshop on Current Knowledge and Research Gaps, 2011

Critical Code: Software Producibility for Defense, 2010
Proceedings of a Workshop on Deterring Cyberattacks: Informing Strategies and Developing Options for U.S. Policy, 2010
Achieving Effective Acquisition of Information Technology in the Department of Defense, 2010

Limited copies of CSTB reports are available free of charge from:
Computer Science and Telecommunications Board
National Research Council
The Keck Center of the National Academies
500 Fifth Street, NW, Washington, DC 20001
(202) 334-2605/cstb@nas.edu
www.cstb.org

**COMMITTEE TO REVIEW THE ENTERPRISE ARCHITECTURE, SOFTWARE DEVELOPMENT APPROACH, AND SAFETY AND HUMAN FACTOR DESIGN OF THE NEXT GENERATION AIR TRANSPORTATION SYSTEM**

DAVID E. LIDDLE, U.S. Venture Partners, *Chair*
STEVEN M. BELLOVIN, Columbia University
JOHN-PAUL B. CLARKE, Georgia Institute of Technology
GEORGE L. DONOHUE, George Mason University
R. JOHN HANSMAN, JR., Massachusetts Institute of Technology
MATS P.E. HEIMDAHL, University of Minnesota, Twin Cities
JOHN C. KNIGHT, University of Virginia
LEON J. OSTERWEIL, University of Massachusetts, Amherst
WALKER E. ROYCE, International Business Machines Corporation
GAVRIEL SALVENDY, Purdue University
THOMAS B. SHERIDAN, Massachusetts Institute of Technology
ROBERT F. SPROULL, University of Massachusetts, Amherst
JAMES W. STURGES, Independent Consultant, Greer, South Carolina
ELAINE WEYUKER, Independent Consultant, Metuchen, New Jersey

*Staff*

LYNETTE I. MILLETT, Associate Director and Senior Program Officer, Computer Science and Telecommunications Board (CSTB)
VIRGINIA BACON TALATI, Program Officer, CSTB
DWAYNE DAY, Senior Program Officer, Aeronautics and Space Engineering Board
JON EISENBERG, Director, CSTB
ERIC WHITAKER, Senior Program Assistant (until March 2015)

## COMPUTER SCIENCE AND TELECOMMUNICATIONS BOARD

ROBERT F. SPROULL, University of Massachusetts, Amherst, *Chair*
LUIZ ANDRE BARROSO, Google, Inc.
ROBERT F. BRAMMER, Brammer Technology, LLC
EDWARD FRANK, Apple, Inc.
SEYMOUR E. GOODMAN, Georgia Institute of Technology
LAURA HAAS, IBM Corporation
MARK HOROWITZ, Stanford University
FARNAM JAHANIAN, Carnegie Mellon University
MICHAEL KEARNS, University of Pennsylvania
ROBERT KRAUT, Carnegie Mellon University
SUSAN LANDAU, Google, Inc.
PETER LEE, Microsoft Corporation
DAVID E. LIDDLE, US Venture Partners
BARBARA LISKOV, Massachusetts Institute of Technology
FRED B. SCHNEIDER, Cornell University
JOHN STANKOVIC, University of Virginia
JOHN A. SWAINSON, Dell, Inc.
PETER SZOLOVITS, Massachusetts Institute of Technology
ERNEST J. WILSON, University of Southern California
KATHERINE YELICK, University of California, Berkeley

*Staff*

JON EISENBERG, Director
LYNETTE I. MILLETT, Associate Director and Senior Program Officer
VIRGINIA BACON TALATI, Program Officer
SHENAE BRADLEY, Senior Program Assistant
EMILY GRUMBLING, Program Officer
RENEE HAWKINS, Financial and Administrative Manager
HERBERT S. LIN, Chief Scientist, *Emeritus*

For more information on CSTB,
see its website at http://www.cstb.org, write to CSTB,
National Research Council, 500 Fifth Street, NW, Washington, DC 20001,
call (202) 334-2605, or e-mail the CSTB at cstb@nas.edu.

# Preface

The Next Generation Air Transportation System (NextGen) is an effort begun in 2003 whose goals include improving the capacity, efficiency, and safety of the U.S. air transportation system and also enabling reduction in noise, pollution, and energy use. The Federal Aviation Administration (FAA) and various stakeholders, including equipment providers, airlines, and contractors, are currently implementing both near- and midterm capabilities of this effort.

Section 212 of the FAA Modernization and Reform Act of 2012, Public Law 112-95 (Box 1.1) called for an examination of NextGen's enterprise architecture and related issues by the National Research Council (NRC). The project that was a result of this call was funded by the FAA. The Committee to Review the Enterprise Architecture, Software Development Approach, and Safety and Human Factor Design of the Next Generation Air Transportation System was formed under the auspices of the NRC's Computer Science and Telecommunications Board in collaboration with the Aeronautics and Space Engineering Board in 2012 to conduct the study. The statement of task for the study committee can be found in Box 1.2.

The committee released a brief interim report in 2014,[1] providing a discussion around the challenges of system architecture for software-intensive systems.

---

[1] National Research Council, *Interim Report of a Review of the Next Generation Air Transportation System Enterprise Architecture, Software, Safety, and Human Factors*, The National Academies Press, Washington, D.C., 2014.

For its final report, the committee received a number of briefings on NextGen efforts, particularly as related to the study's focus on enterprise architecture, software development approach, and safety and human factors. A list of briefers at committee meetings can be found in Appendix B. Subsets of the committee also conducted several informal site visits to gain insight on the system development process and FAA's technical research. A subset of the committee visited the FAA's William J. Hughes Technical Center in Atlantic City, New Jersey, and heard briefings on human factors research, test and evaluation processes, and cybersecurity considerations. Several members of the committee also met with experts at Lockheed Martin and Raytheon to learn generally about contractors' software development practices and to better understand FAA's approach to and expectations regarding system integration. Additionally, during the committee's work, MITRE was completing an independent assessment of NextGen at the request of the FAA and provided an overview of its work and process to the committee. The committee appreciates the insights of the individuals at these organizations who participated in those meetings and especially thanks Andy Anderegg, MITRE; Fran Hill, Lockheed Martin; Charles Keegan, Raytheon; and Kaye Jackson, FAA, for helping to facilitate those visits.

As discussed in this report, there have been a number of definitional and terminological challenges encountered in the course of this study. The committee addresses a number of issues, such as a fluid definition of the NextGen project, the comingling of normal modernization efforts with more transformational developments, and an administrative rather than technical architectural standard. Those issues at times temporarily masked deep and critical issues with which the committee had to grapple to reach meaningful findings and recommendations. We are indebted to the staff of the Next Generation Program Office and their FAA colleagues for their patient efforts on behalf of the study committee in striving to clarify these issues.

David E. Liddle, *Chair*
Committee to Review the Enterprise Architecture, Software Development Approach, and Safety and Human Factor Design of the Next Generation Air Transportation System

# Acknowledgment of Reviewers

This report has been reviewed in draft form by individuals chosen for their diverse perspectives and technical expertise, in accordance with procedures approved by the National Research Council's Report Review Committee. The purpose of this independent review is to provide candid and critical comments that will assist the institution in making its published report as sound as possible and to ensure that the report meets institutional standards for objectivity, evidence, and responsiveness to the study charge. The review comments and draft manuscript remain confidential to protect the integrity of the deliberative process. We wish to thank the following individuals for their review of this report:

ELLA ATKINS, University of Michigan,
ARNOLD BARNETT, Massachusetts Institute of Technology,
RICHARD BERMAN, LICAS,
KARL HEDRICK, University of California, Berkeley,
RICHARD HILLIARD, Independent Consultant,
BUTLER LAMPSON, Microsoft Research,
JOHN LAUBER, Airbus, SAS (retired),
STEVEN LIPNER, Microsoft Corporation (retired),
BARBARA LISKOV, Massachusetts Institute of Technology,
MARK MAIER, Aerospace Corporation,
WILLIAM SCHERLIS, Carnegie Mellon University,
AGAM SINHA, ANS Aviation International,
RAYMOND VALEIKA, Delta Airlines, Inc., and
STEVE WINTER, Raytheon.

Although the reviewers listed above have provided many constructive comments and suggestions, they were not asked to endorse the conclusions or recommendations, nor did they see the final draft of the report before its release. The review of this report was overseen by Ali Mosleh, University of California, Los Angeles. Appointed by the National Research Council, he was responsible for making certain that an independent examination of this report was carried out in accordance with institutional procedures and that all review comments were carefully considered. Responsibility for the final content of this report rests entirely with the authoring committee and the institution.

# Contents

SUMMARY                                                                          1

1   RECOGNIZE CONSTRAINTS AND ALIGN EXPECTATIONS      13
    Scope of Report, 14
    What is NextGen—Aligning Expectations, 17

2   ASSERT ARCHITECTURAL LEADERSHIP                              24
    FAA's Current Approach to Architecture, 25
    Elements of Architectural Leadership, 40
    Recommendations to Improve Architecture and Architectural
        Leadership, 43

3   COPE WITH CHANGE                                                           49
    Cybersecurity, 49
    Unmanned Aircraft Systems, 53
    Safety in NextGen and Emergent System Properties, 56
    Risk Management, 58

4   MINIMIZE CULTURAL AND ORGANIZATIONAL BARRIERS   64
    Human Factors, 65
    Costs and Benefits, 71
    The Challenge of Being a System Integrator, 74
    Support for Operations and Maintenance, 78

APPENDIXES

| | | |
|---|---|---|
| A | Biographies of Committee Members and Staff | 83 |
| B | Briefers to the Study Committee | 93 |
| C | Acronyms | 95 |

# Summary

Section 212 of the Federal Aviation Administration Modernization and Reform Act of 2012, Public Law 112-95, calls for an examination by the National Research Council (NRC) of the Next Generation Air Transportation System's (NextGen's) enterprise software development approach and safety and human factor design. In response to this request, the NRC formed the Committee to Review the Enterprise Architecture, Software Development Approach, and Safety and Human Factor Design of the Next Generation Air Transportation System to conduct this study.

The committee's overarching conclusions are as follows: The original vision for NextGen is not what is being implemented today. Instead, NextGen today primarily emphasizes replacing and modernizing aging equipment and systems. This shift in focus has not been clear to all stakeholders. Nevertheless, modernization is critical, and large-scale, software-intensive systems such as NextGen require ongoing support for operations and maintenance.

To be successful, even as a modernization project, NextGen needs a system architecture that defines how the pieces of the system fit together and allows for modeling and reasoning about possible futures. The existing National Airspace System (NAS) enterprise architecture is not that; it primarily documents existing systems and plans. Among other things, a system architecture is an essential tool for managing risk. The Federal Aviation Administration (FAA) should create an architecture community that can produce and evolve a system architecture and should also strengthen its workforce in systems engineering and integration, digital communications, and cybersecurity to increase the likelihood it will succeed in developing the architecture and managing the implementation of the systems it describes.

NextGen and its system architecture should be developed to cope with change. Two newly important areas, cybersecurity and unmanned vehicles, make this need particularly resonant. Human factors will also play an important role in NextGen and the NAS as each evolves. Finally, regarding anticipated costs and benefits, airlines are not motivated to spend money on equipment and training for NextGen because they do not receive most of the benefits directly and because of implementation schedule uncertainties. The rest of this summary elaborates these and related observations in more detail and highlights several of the committee's findings and recommendations in bold.

## ALIGNING EXPECTATIONS FOR NEXTGEN

Throughout the committee's work, it became clear that "NextGen" means different things to different people, ranging from a wide-ranging transformational vision to a much more concrete set of phased incremental changes to various parts of the NAS. With so many stakeholders and so many moving parts, different understandings of "what is NextGen" arose. As the committee has come to understand it, NextGen today is a set of programs to implement a suite of incremental changes to the NAS. Although some technologies and/or systems will be new, in most cases, current plans call for them to be used to closely replicate existing capabilities (such as satellite navigation used to replace radar functionality rather than the reinvention of flight).

The executive order establishing the Joint Planning and Development Office (JPDO) was entitled "Transformation of the National Air Transportation System,"[1] and early vision documents referred to ambitious goals such as integrated data streams for situational awareness in seamless multi-agency global operations, scalability, the use of emerging space-based communications and surveillance technologies.[2] Although progress has been made, not all parts of the original JPDO vision will be achieved in the foreseeable future. This was true even at the outset of NextGen and is understandable, given changes over time.[3] However, even

---

[1] White House, "Transformation of the National Air Transportation System," Executive Order, released November 18, 2008, http://georgewbush-whitehouse.archives.gov/news/releases/2008/11/20081118.html.

[2] See Appendix B of the 2005 National Research Council report *Technology Pathways: Assessing the Integrated Plan for a Next Generation Air Transportation System* (The National Academies Press, Washington, D.C.) for an overview of JPDO objectives.

[3] For instance, the substantial future demand growth anticipated in early planning did not materialize.

the limited vision embraced at the start of NextGen has been reduced over time, while increasingly important challenges have not received adequate attention.[4] Partly as a result of these issues, stakeholder expectations for NextGen have become misaligned with current planning as NextGen and its constituent programs have changed over time. This misalignment causes challenges both for the FAA and for stakeholders.

An important part of NextGen is addressing the need to replace aging equipment. Such modernization is essential and important. Replacing or upgrading systems while continuously and safely operating the whole system is an intricate undertaking, a process that the FAA seems to have mastered. The successful operation of such systems requires ongoing alterations and improvements, not just the occasional repair of faulty equipment and software. While not the transformation originally envisioned for NextGen, continuing to refresh the technology-driven systems is necessary for safety critical systems like the NAS.

As described to the committee, NextGen also includes efforts to further deploy performance-based navigation,[5] redesign certain aspects of the airspace, and equip aircraft with technology (such as Automatic Dependent Surveillance-Broadcast (ADS-B) that can form the basis for future capabilities, along with a broad range of activities. These plans are expressed in various implementation plans, the NAS enterprise architecture, roadmaps, and calls for research, experimentation, and further incremental programs. NextGen, as currently executed, is not, however, broadly transformational. That is, it does not set out a series of planned steps toward a fundamentally transformed end-state (such as free flight, decommissioning surveillance radar stations, automating air traffic control processes with a completely digital information infrastructure, or shifting authority from ground to air). Moreover, the system has not been significantly changed to take advantage of available information and communications technologies or to enable major improvements in how the airspace can be organized and managed. Unfortunately, over the course of the committee's work, it was clear that some stakeholders were still anticipating these capabilities from NextGen. Such goals await the now-distant full deployment of technical capabilities, the integration of these capabilities to support higher levels of automation and more distributed and autonomous operation, full equipage of virtually all aircraft with new components, and widespread revisions to procedures. "NextGen" has become a misnomer.

---

[4] For instance, cybersecurity was not a significant concern in early JPDO planning.

[5] Performance-based navigation refers to a range of approaches that emphasize the performance and capabilities of aircraft over more conventional ground-based navigation systems.

**Recommendation: The Federal Aviation Administration (FAA), Congress, and all National Airspace System stakeholders should reset expectations for the Next Generation Air Transportation System. The FAA should explicitly qualify the early transformational vision in a way that clearly articulates the new realities.**

The committee's conclusion that NextGen today is primarily an incremental modernization effort should not suggest that NextGen therefore has an obvious completed state or that future significant change should not happen. Given the continuing rapid pace of technological evolution and ongoing changes in what is demanded of the NAS, the NextGen effort is properly seen as an ongoing process, punctuated by particular efforts focused on particular capabilities. Resetting expectations with a clear baseline will provide a useful foundation on which to build.

## ASSERTING ARCHITECTURAL LEADERSHIP

The statement of task for this study (Box 1.2) uses the term "enterprise architecture." Like other terms associated with software-intensive systems, this term is used in different ways by different organizations and in different contexts, but typically, an enterprise architecture serves as documentation and support of existing systems and business processes. An enterprise architecture alone cannot usually manage large, distributed, real-time systems where safety-critical concerns predominate, nor is it clear that even the best instantiation of an enterprise architecture is intended for such uses. An enterprise architecture is typically interpreted as a set of documents instead of a set of decisions. This is consistent with what the committee learned in its briefings about the FAA's approach to enterprise architecture. However, a focus on documentation over decision making is a significant problem.

For a system such as NextGen, a more comprehensive notion of architecture is needed. A system architecture, by contrast with an enterprise architecture, models and defines the structure and behavior of a system in a way that supports reasoning about the system and its characteristics. Accordingly, and consistent with other elements of its task, such as software development, the committee explored the question of architecture more broadly, focusing also on the system architecture for NextGen.

Discerning precisely what FAA's architectural approach and strategy is was challenging, and some of it had to be inferred. The current enterprise architecture as presented to the committee appears to be a set of functional enclaves that are providing individual services, described in a set of documents at the NAS enterprise architecture level. Additional improvements and modifications seem to be either changes to what is already deployed or overlays onto what is already there.

Ultimately, the committee's conclusion with regard to the NAS enterprise architecture is that the existing design and deployment of the NAS embodies a tacit architecture—the de facto system architecture is the system as it is today. This induced architecture is therefore bottom-up and program-driven and imposes implicit limits on what (and how) system capabilities can be realized. This has ramifications for how effective it can be, especially in laying groundwork for future flexibility and enhancements.

A tacit architecture is not appropriate for a system of NextGen's scale and importance and is at odds with recommendations in standards such as ISO/IEC/IEEE 42010.[6] FAA's approach to architecture (which focuses on the enterprise architecture) is not an adequate technical foundation for steering NextGen's technical governance and managing the inevitable changes in technology and operations.

The changes to the NAS envisioned under the NextGen umbrella should provoke changes and adjustments in the NAS system architecture. Change can be thought of as the ongoing management of trade-offs, which are not clearly identified in the existing tacit architecture. That tacit architecture is diffused through many different programs, not all of which are under NextGen control. A system architecture for the NAS should help ensure proper operation of the system and allow proper analyses for prediction of system behavior and performance and ensure future evolvability. Absent such an architecture, whether NextGen can meet its stated objectives and requirements is unknown and, probably, unknowable. That the system architecture is not well developed is hard to discern because of the nearly exclusive focus by the FAA on the enterprise architecture.

Unfortunately, having de facto established the existing (baseline) architecture as *the* architecture without a clear architectural expression of future expectations regarding change, trade-offs, and evolvability, many opportunities to use the architecture in forward-looking ways have been ruled out, and some important advances are going to be extremely challenging to accomplish (such as the ability to create persuasive and credible forecasts of change costs, technical risks, capability upgrades, and performance improvements). The committee's recommendations take this into account and offer suggestions as to how to move forward most productively to develop better architectural approaches.

The most important thing on which the FAA should focus with respect to architecture is building a community of architecture leaders within and

---

[6] International Organization for Standardization (ISO)/International Electrotechnical Commission (IEC)/Institute of Electrical and Electronics Engineers (IEEE), Standard ISO/IEC/IEEE 42010:2011, "Systems and Software Engineering—Architecture Description," December 2011, http://www.iso.org/iso/catalogue_detail.htm?csnumber=50508.

outside the agency. The FAA will need to add more system architecture skill and establish a more capable architecture community. Architectural leadership should encompass multiple perspectives (including, but not limited to, the enterprise architecture) and provide diversity of thought and approach, emphasizing flexibility and evolvability, consistency and alignment, and right-sizing of architectural documentation. To be clear, the committee does not urge the premature creation of more detailed specifications and artifacts absent deeper insights and stronger analyses of risks and trade-offs. In many ways, such efforts would be counterproductive, translating into more overhead (process and documentation) and less attention, resources, and expertise focused on better design, decisions, tests, and earlier integration.

Like other federal agencies, the FAA faces challenges in implementing information technology systems and in recruiting and retaining the workforce needed for designing, maintaining, and enhancing systems such as NextGen. In particular, the FAA is ill-equipped to perform as a systems integrator. If the FAA is to succeed in both the medium and long term, it will require enhancements to its technical expertise. Architecture and systems engineering, which are needed for successful integration of capabilities and platforms into a coherent NAS system, have been undervalued. Program management and systems engineering process are important, but are not a substitute for talent that can effectively guide the design and evolution of NextGen. Even if the FAA were not acting as systems integrator, it would still need to be a "smart customer"—it needs expertise that will enable it to effectively structure and manage its supplier relationships.

Today, the FAA relies greatly on its vendors and other external talent. For architectural insight and expertise internally, it depends on a very small number of individuals and lacks the critical mass that characterizes a vibrant and effective technical community. Digital communications will take on increasing importance as the NAS is modernized, so the FAA will need additional technical expertise in designing modern digital networks and protocols. Cybersecurity is a challenge facing all who use modern computing and communications technology, and the potential threats and risks are magnified for critical infrastructure like the NAS. The FAA needs strong cybersecurity expertise in designing, implementing, integrating, and operating NextGen systems. Cybersecurity requires a system-wide approach and cannot be addressed piecemeal by each contractor (or program) separately.

**Recommendation: The Federal Aviation Administration (FAA) should nurture workforce talent in the areas of systems engineering, architecture, systems integration, digital communications, and**

cybersecurity. Significant effort will be required to attract, develop, and retain this talent, given the high demand outside the FAA.

Recommendation: The Federal Aviation Administration (FAA) should initiate, grow, and engage a capable architecture community—leaders and peers within and outside the FAA—who will expand the breadth and depth of expertise that is steering architectural changes.

Recommendation: The Federal Aviation Administration should conduct a small number of experiments among its system integration partners to prototype candidate solutions for establishing and managing a vibrant architectural community.

Recommendation: Should the Federal Aviation Administration continue to act as the systems integrator of Next Generation Air Transportation System programs, it should maintain architectural leadership and not delegate architecture definition and control to contractors.

Recommendation: The Federal Aviation Administration should use an architecture leadership community and an effective governance approach to assure a proper balance between documents and artifacts and to provide high-level guidance and a capability that (1) enables effective management and communication of dependencies, (2) provides flexibility and evolvability to ensure accommodation of future needs, and (3) communicates changing circumstances in order to align expectations.

## OPERATIONS AND MAINTENANCE

A common fallacy with software-intensive systems is that they can be built, deployed, and then operated with relatively little "maintenance" and modernization effort. The surprise, for those unfamiliar with such systems, is that operations and maintenance will very often include substantial modernization effort. This effort is needed both in response to new requirements and also in response to rapid growth and change in technological infrastructure. This is true for NextGen and the NAS, and this fact has implications for how the FAA should explain its needs to Congress and its overseers. Although Congress has been supportive of FAA efforts, in the committee's view, there is a specific need for support of ongoing maintenance and modernization (upgrades), including refreshing and modernizing both the hardware and software so as to provide reliable, cost-effective operation. A typical pattern in government is that funds are allocated for specific (new) programs or projects without sufficient allocation for out-year maintenance or for maintenance and refresh of existing (and still important) programs. Modernizing software is just as important to safety and operational efficiency as modernizing hardware.

> **Finding: As a large-scale, software-intensive system, NextGen and the NAS will benefit if ongoing maintenance of the NAS and its hardware and software systems are supported—in addition to programmatic investments; such an approach will make the most of past and ongoing investments.**

## MANAGING RISK

The risks and uncertainties in NextGen are inherently difficult to quantify. However, quantifying risks and value offers means for better planning and management. The challenge for complex systems such as NextGen is not how to eliminate risks but rather how to manage them successfully. In all engineering projects, and particularly software engineering projects, this usually means understanding the consequences of risky decisions as early in the life cycle as possible, lest the costs of unwinding previous bad decisions become prohibitive, and the architecture becomes a source of change friction that burdens efficiency of execution. By contrast, an effective architecture can be a basis for risk assessment and mitigation and can be used as a tool to support decision making and the recording of decisions.

NextGen today embodies a set of (often implicit) decisions to not dramatically change a wide range of current operations. Those decisions, along with an analysis of their implications, are not explicit in the tacit architecture. But a decision to not change carries heavy implications for the realization of any gains that would require such changes. To cope well with uncertainty and risk, it is important to explicitly state value attributes (with scales), to develop multiple alternative architectures, and to have evaluation models that compare those alternatives to the value attributes. The committee was struck by the lack of alternatives analysis in NextGen. Nor is there a well-specified overview of what is and is not known about the value of various proposed levels of change (e.g., partial deployment of certain technologies or features).

Schedule risks in NextGen have multiple sources, including budget, approval, certification, and procedure design. With the exception of resourcing and budgets, architecture can help mitigate these. However, a poorly developed system architecture makes it a challenge to determine how well the overall system will address system requirements (e.g., for security and robustness), causing risks of many kinds, including schedule risks. The risks to NextGen are not clearly articulated or quantified in order of importance, making it difficult to make sound decisions about how to prioritize efforts and allocate resources.

> **Recommendation: The Federal Aviation Administration should use an architecture leadership community and a system architecture, with input from specialists in probability and statistics, as key tools in managing and mitigating risks and in assessing new value opportunities.**

## COPING WITH CHANGE

The national airspace is a critical infrastructure for the United States. In concert with revising the architectural approach for NextGen, plans to cope with unanticipated change are needed. Indeed, any architectures developed must themselves reflect planning for resilience. Cybersecurity, safety, and unmanned aircraft systems (UAS) illustrate why planning for resilience in NextGen and in the NextGen system architecture is so important. UAS were not explicitly anticipated in NextGen. And cybersecurity by its very nature demands constant adaptation to a dynamic threat environment.

NextGen is no exception to modern cybersecurity risks and threats; indeed, the safety of life implications and the vital economic importance of air travel make the security of NextGen and the NAS critically important. As various programs and components of the national airspace are modernized, the security implications of the changes will need to be taken into account. The criticality of cybersecurity for NextGen increases as more services rely on digital technologies, networked communications, and commercial-off-the-shelf software. Cybersecurity challenges extend from major software platforms into the specification and design of embedded (avionics) equipment that connects directly to the NAS. Although there will always be risk, the lack of appropriate architectural approaches to security and safety that allow for reasoning about risks, and uncertainty only increase the likelihood that risks of unknown magnitude can remain embedded in the NAS.

The committee's impression from briefings and discussion with the FAA is that cybersecurity, although acknowledged as an issue with some efforts under way to address it, has not been fully integrated into the agency's thinking, planning, and efforts with respect to NextGen and the NAS generally. In particular, as new technologies and procedures are rolled out, there will inevitably be new vulnerabilities. Moreover, changes in the way existing, long-stable technologies are used may introduce new security issues. So threat analyses both on existing systems, with any expected changes, and on new components are needed. Cybersecurity will need to be an important and integral part of safety activities and is an ongoing operational matter (not only a question of design and architecture).

> **Recommendation: The Federal Aviation Administration (FAA) should incorporate cybersecurity as a systems characteristic at all levels of the architecture and design.** The FAA should begin by developing a threat model followed by an appropriate set of architectural and design concepts that will mitigate the associated risks, support resilience in the face of attack or compromise, and allow for dynamic evolution to meet a changing threat environment. The FAA should inculcate a cybersecurity mindset complementary to its well-established safety mindset throughout the organization, its contractors, and leadership.

UAS are already in use as hobbyist craft, and the FAA estimates that thousands of small UAS could be active over the next 5 years. Several NextGen technologies are essential to the safe integration of UAS: the NAS voice system, which will allow UAS pilots to communicate with air traffic control over ground-to-ground communication networks; Data Communications (Data Comm), which will support the transmission of digital messages to the flight crew; and System Wide Information Management (SWIM), which will support more timely and improved information access to all users of the NAS.

However, NextGen planning and architecture did not explicitly anticipate the introduction of UAS and thus does not readily lend itself to incorporating these new types of aircraft that will place new demands on the system. The challenge of integrating UAS into the national airspace illustrates the challenges of accommodating changing requirements within the current approach to managing architectural and system evolution. The expected integration of UAS into the NAS will present new safety issues stemming from increased reliance on data links, limited operator sensory and environmental cues, and so on. An insufficiently developed system architecture is one of several obstacles to introducing UAS into the NAS. The integration of UAS is an example of a rapidly emerging requirement that could provoke disruptive changes to both technology and to roles and responsibilities.

Per its charge, the committee's focus has been on architecture, especially system architecture. The committee urges the FAA to use UAS as a use case for developing a better approach to system architecture (and associated technical and procedural designs). One measure of the quality of the NAS system architecture is (and will be) its flexibility in addressing UAS operations as they unfold, recognizing that UAS requirements and capabilities are likely to change a great deal as these technologies mature.

**Recommendation: The Federal Aviation Administration (FAA) and its architecture leadership community should look for and apply lessons from the challenge of integrating unmanned aircraft systems (UAS) into the National Airspace System (NAS) as it develops an effective system architecture. The FAA and its architecture leadership community should incorporate measures in the NAS system architecture to address UAS integration.**

## INCORPORATING HUMAN FACTORS

The medium-term plans for the NAS will not fundamentally change the roles and activities of pilots and controllers. However, even with modest changes, misunderstandings and errors can result. Numerous constraints challenge the ability of the FAA to smoothly and effectively make changes to its systems and procedures. Furthermore, human factors for crew and controllers alike are an important ingredient in successful changes. Procedures and airspace redesign go hand-in-hand with technical changes and adjustments and are often just as complicated—and thus a bottleneck to realizing expected benefits of new technologies and approaches.

Human factors need to be incorporated in design, technical, engineering, and architectural discussions as early as possible, not after the design is complete (e.g., as a check on the design). This is both an organizational challenge for the FAA—as it may not have sufficient human factors personnel to integrate contractors' work with system design—as well as a technical and engineering challenge—determining how requirements and constraints flow to early stage technical requirements, so that human factors perspectives can contribute to early design work. When human factors are not included at the outset, products and services need to be modified subsequently to meet the human factors requirements, which delays the release of products and services and significantly increases cost.

**Recommendation: The Federal Aviation Administration (FAA) should recognize and incorporate in early design phases the human factors and procedural and airspace implications of stated goals and associated technical changes. In addition, the FAA should ensure that a human factors specialist, separate from the research and certification groups, has sign-off authority within the Next Generation Air Transportation System approval process.**

## ASSESSING COSTS AND BENEFITS

As part of its charge, the committee also explored anticipated costs and benefits to NextGen and their implications. The FAA has put forward a business case for NextGen,[7] and the committee held several discussions with FAA staff as well to understand the analysis used to develop the costs and benefits of implementing NextGen.

NextGen plans require a substantial investment, both by the taxpayer via the FAA for infrastructure, and by carriers and aircraft owners for equipage and training. At best, benefits—however quantified—to carriers will lag deployment costs; and benefits that accrue to the carriers will be less than the projected social benefits (quantified in the form of reduced delays to passengers, as is standard for Department of Transportation analyses of this sort) to the system as a whole. Many of the benefits of NextGen, such as those enabled by increased automatic communication between aircraft, cannot be meaningfully realized unless air carriers each equip their fleets with the requisite technology and, indeed, depend on all or nearly all aircraft being so equipped. The carriers will also incur training costs, both for new equipage and for new procedures that use old equipage. For airlines to gain significant benefit, NextGen capabilities will need to be deployed at sufficient scale. Given the delay in implementing new procedures and technologies at major airports, airlines may not see benefits for some time. The costs and benefits analysis presented to the committee was sensible; however, that mismatch presents an ongoing challenge for the FAA and Congress. Current short- and medium-term goals for NextGen emphasize new technologies to improve and enhance existing capabilities. Although modernization efforts are important and can bring significant benefits, it remains a challenge to incentivize uptake (e.g., equipage, training, or changes in procedures) absent clear benefits.

**Recommendation: Preceding any further equipage mandate, the Federal Aviation Administration (FAA) should provide an estimated statement of costs and benefits that is mutually reviewed and agreed upon with the relevant stakeholders. It should be based on a mature and stable technical specification and a committed timeline for FAA deliverables and investment (for procedure and airspace design, infrastructure deployment, training, and so on). On this basis, industry could responsibly invest as required, given a reasonable expected return.**

---

[7] Federal Aviation Administration, *The Business Case for the Next Generation Air Transportation System: FY 2013*, Washington, D.C., 2013.

# 1

# Recognize Constraints and Align Expectations

In 2003, an effort to transform the U.S. air transportation system was announced and the Joint Planning and Development Office (JPDO) was established by Congress to develop the Next Generation Air Transportation System (NextGen).[1] NextGen refers to a set of programs and initiatives to be coordinated into an evolving overall air transportation system aimed at a continuing transformation of the National Airspace System (NAS).[2] NextGen aims to overhaul the U.S. air transportation system through a combination of procedural and technological improvements. It is intended to make use of extant capabilities along with newer enabling technologies such as precision satellite navigation systems and a digital communications infrastructure to share real-time information. Effective use of these tools could make it possible to shorten routes, navigate better around weather, save time and fuel, reduce delays, increase capacity at airports not already capacity-limited by physical infrastructure, and improve capabilities for monitoring and managing of aircraft. The Federal Aviation Administration

---

[1] The Joint Planning and Development Office (JPDO) was a multi-agency initiative created to oversee planning and coordination for NextGen. In 2014, funding for the JPDO was eliminated, and the FAA created a new Interagency Planning Office to replace it. See reporting on a statement FAA provided to AIN at B. Carey, "FAA's New 'Interagency Planning Office' Replaces JPDO," *AIN Online*, May 27, 2014, http://www.ainonline.com/aviation-news/air-transport/2014-05-27/faas-new-interagency-planning-office-replaces-jpdo.

[2] NextGen and other programs or initiatives of similar scale are sometimes referred to as "systems of systems." Any system of systems is itself a system, and the committee has chosen in this report to use the term "system" for simplicity.

(FAA), working along with a wide range of stakeholders, is currently working toward both near-term and midterm capabilities.[3]

Section 212 of the Federal Aviation Administration Modernization and Reform Act of 2012, Public Law 112-95 (see Box 1.1), calls for an examination by the National Research Council (NRC) of NextGen's enterprise software development approach and safety and human factors design. To respond to this request, the NRC formed the Committee to Review the Enterprise Architecture, Software Development Approach, and Safety and Human Factor Design of the Next Generation Air Transportation System in 2012 to conduct this study. In this final report, the committee provides its analysis and recommendations to the FAA with a particular focus on the importance of system architecture and its implications.

## SCOPE OF REPORT

The committee was asked to address a broad suite of topics related to NextGen. The material in this chapter provides context and background on NextGen and provides some of the committee's observations about how NextGen has, and has not, developed over time. Drawing on the technical expertise and experience of its members, the committee chose to use system architecture as an organizing principle through which to assess the input it received, to organize its recommendations, and to address its statement of task (Box 1.2). Chapter 2 explains this in detail. Point 1 of the statement of task asks the committee to consider a variety of factors with respect to transitioning to the future system envisioned by the JPDO. As described, that vision has been overtaken by subsequent events that took place before the committee first convened.

Accordingly, the committee discusses those factors as they relate to NextGen currently. Safety issues are discussed in Chapter 3, and human factors are discussed in Chapter 4. Point 2 of the statement of task asks the committee to consider risk, benefits, and software development. These topics are addressed in Chapter 4. Point 3 of the statement of task asks the committee to consider risks of automation and apply lessons from other entities. As noted above, NextGen as currently planned will not have significant amounts of new automation (as was envisioned by the early JPDO). Chapters 2, 3, and 4 offer the committee's recommendations to the FAA on how to better manage planning and risk based on the committee members' experiences in a variety of other domains.

---

[3] More information about NextGen can be found in the NextGen Implementation Plan, on the Federal Aviation Administration's (FAA's) website at http://www.faa.gov/nextgen/library/.

> **BOX 1.1 Section 212 of the FAA Modernization and Reform Act of 2012, Public Law 112-95**
>
> SEC. 212. EXPERT REVIEW OF ENTERPRISE ARCHITECTURE FOR NEXTGEN.
>
> (a) REVIEW.—The Administrator of the Federal Aviation Administration shall enter into an arrangement with the National Research Council to review the enterprise architecture for the NextGen.
>
> (b) CONTENTS.—At a minimum, the review to be conducted under subsection (a) shall—
>
> (1) highlight the technical activities, including human-system design, organizational design, and other safety and human factor aspects of the system, that will be necessary to successfully transition current and planned modernization programs to the future system envisioned by the Joint Planning and Development Office of the Administration;
> (2) assess technical, cost, and schedule risk for the software development that will be necessary to achieve the expected benefits from a highly automated air traffic management system and the implications for ongoing modernization projects; and
> (3) determine how risks with automation efforts for the NextGen can be mitigated based on the experiences of other public or private entities in developing complex, software-intensive systems.
>
> (c) REPORT.—Not later than 1 year after the date of enactment of this Act, the Administrator shall submit to the Committee on Transportation and Infrastructure of the House of Representatives and the Committee on Commerce, Science, and Transportation of the Senate a report containing the results of the review conducted pursuant to subsection (a).

Questions that are relevant to all of these issues concern how the FAA should be organized, what its funding structure should be, and what governance structure is most appropriate for the agency as a whole. The committee believes there is much to be learned from exploring these questions, and they do bear significantly on planning and architecture for NextGen. However, that exploration was beyond the scope of this committee's tasking, and thus the report does not address these questions directly.

During the course of this study, there were numerous other efforts under way related to NextGen planning. The Department of Transportation Inspector General issued a report urging sustained FAA leadership

> **BOX 1.2 Statement of Task**
>
> As stipulated in Sec. 212 of the FAA Modernization and Reform Act of 2012, PL 112-95, a National Research Council study would review the enterprise architecture, software development approach, and safety and human factor design aspects of the Next Generation Air Transportation System (NextGen). An ad hoc committee will conduct a study and prepare a report that will (1) highlight the technical activities, including human-system design and testing, organizational design, and other safety and human factor aspects of the system, that will be necessary to successfully transition current and planned modernization programs to the future system envisioned by the Joint Planning and Development Office of the Administration and obtain necessary certifications and operational approval; (2) assess technical, cost, and schedule risk for the software development that will be necessary to achieve the expected benefits from a highly automated air traffic management system and the implications for ongoing modernization projects; and (3) determine how risks with automation efforts for the NextGen can be mitigated based on the experiences of other public or private entities in developing complex, software-intensive systems, particularly for life-critical, real-time operational systems, and including past aviation system development programs. The committee will issue a brief interim report within 12 months providing an initial assessment focusing on software development challenges and a final report within 18 months providing a full assessment of the issues listed above.

and action to address NextGen delays.[4] The Government Accountability Office also urged substantial leadership commitment and the empowering of leaders to make critical decisions.[5] MITRE's Center for Advanced Aviation Development—FAA's federally funded research and development center—recently recommended six strategic focus areas to move forward with NextGen, the first of which emphasized the importance of transformational and foundational infrastructure.[6] The committee's final report here should be seen as complementary to these, emphasizing the

---

[4] Department of Transportation, *Addressing Underlying Causes for NextGen Delays Will Require Sustained FAA Leadership and Action*, Office of Inspector General Audit Report AV-2014-031, February, 25, 2014, https://www.oig.dot.gov/library-item/28823.

[5] Government Accountability Office, "FAA Reauthorization Act: Progress and Challenges Implementing Various Provisions of the 2012 Act: Statement of Gerald L. Dillingham, PhD, Director, Physical Infrastructure," Testimony Before the Subcommittee on Aviation, Committee on Transportation and Infrastructure, U.S. House of Representatives, GAO-14-285T, February 5, 2014, http://www.gao.gov/assets/670/660683.pdf.

[6] MITRE Corporation, *NextGen Independent Assessment and Recommendations*, MP 140440, October 2014, http://www.faa.gov/nextgen/media/MITRE_NextGen_Independent_Assessment_and_Recommendations.pdf.

importance of system architecture and architectural leadership and drawing connections between architectural choices and broader outcomes.

## WHAT IS NEXTGEN—ALIGNING EXPECTATIONS

Although technological and procedural improvements have been introduced into the NAS over the years to increase capacity, reduce delays, and improve safety, elements of the NAS rely on outdated technology. The system as a whole has not been significantly changed to take advantage of available information and communications technologies that could engender needed improvements in the security, robustness, and evolvability of the NAS and enable major improvements in how the airspace can be organized and managed.

There are numerous complex constraints on the design and operation of the NAS to which the FAA and its stakeholders are subject. The FAA is well aware of these constraints—some of which affect development of systems and some of which affect potential benefits and outcomes. Furthermore, the NAS exists in a complex political, organizational, and economic milieu that imposes its own constraints and demands as well. For example, few airports have the option to build additional runways; aircraft capacity decisions are solely in the hands of the airlines and manufacturers; and alternative competitive intercity transportation options, such as high speed rail or other ground transportation means, do not exist in most major cities—all of which continue to place increased pressure on Metroplex airports.[7] In the committee's view, it is helpful to keep these often challenging constraints, which include legacy commitments already made, in mind when planning, assessing, or evaluating NextGen efforts.

Throughout the committee's work, it became clear that "NextGen" means different things to different people, ranging from a wide-ranging transformational vision to a much more concrete set of phased incremental changes to various parts of the NAS. With so many stakeholders and so many moving parts, different understandings of "what is NextGen" have arisen. The committee has come to a view of what NextGen is (and is not), and that view is described briefly below for the purposes of this report. Any particular definition is less important, however, than ensuring that all stakeholders understand each other's expectations and

---

[7] *Metroplex* refers to "a system of airports in close proximity and their shared airspace that serve one or more major cities. A metroplex has at least one, but often two or more major commercial airports." They include the following: Atlanta, Boston, Charlotte, Chicago, Cleveland, Washington, D.C., Denver, Detroit, Houston, Las Vegas Valley, Memphis, Minneapolis-St. Paul, New York/Philadelphia, North Texas, Northern California, Orlando, Phoenix, Seattle, South Florida, Southern California, and Tampa. See FAA, "Metroplexes," last modified August 26, 2014, http://www.faa.gov/Nextgen/snapshots/metroplexes/.

anticipated outcomes and that capabilities, plans, and requirements are aligned well.

The vision and concept of operation for NextGen was set forth in documents from JPDO. In particular, a 2004 Concept of Operations described at a very high level a desired end state for the NAS, and that description was developed in more detail in later versions.[8] Briefings and documents provided to the committee have indicated the capabilities expected to be deployed in the "medium term" (a time frame defined by the FAA as "by 2018"). These plans call for the execution of several programs that provide new or replacement technology.

For example, Automatic Dependent Surveillance-Broadcast (ADS-B) provides a new, Global Positioning System (GPS)-based surveillance capability complementing and partially replacing existing surveillance radars.[9] En Route Automation Modernization (ERAM) replaces the En Route Host computer system with new display, communications, and planning tools for air traffic controllers. An enhanced data communications system (Data Comm) will allow for incremental replacement of data-intensive communications between air traffic control and the flight crew with digital communications (such as transmitting flight plans to aircraft). The System Wide Information Management (SWIM) system enables the sharing of real-time digital information between different systems and stakeholders, such as carriers, airports, aircraft maintenance operators, and so on. Other programs relating to weather support services, air traffic management, and voice systems are also under way to support NextGen goals.

The existing documents and decisions specify solutions and technology but not operations. A standard good practice is that operations should be carefully defined independent of technological implementation. This is particularly important where value improvement comes from operational changes. New technologies under consideration imply changed operations to realize large value, but the FAA has not addressed this through a detailed operational analysis. Standard practice is that the "owning" organization should play close attention to the operational description

---

[8] See Chapter 4 of JPDO, *Next Generation Air Transportation System Integrated Plan*, 2004, http://www.dtic.mil/dtic/tr/fulltext/u2/a605269.pdf; JPDO, *Making the NextGen Vision a Reality: 2006 Progress Report to the Next Generation Air Transportation System Integrated Plan*, 2006, http://www.dtic.mil/dtic/tr/fulltext/u2/a502356.pdf; and JPDO, Version 2.0, 2007, http://www.dtic.mil/dtic/tr/fulltext/u2/a496134.pdf; JPDO Concept of Operations for the Next Generation Air Transportation System Draft 3 Version 1.1a, December 6, 2006; FAA NextGen Mid-Term Concept of Operations for the National Airspace System, Version 2.0, April 30, 2010.

[9] Automatic dependent surveillance-broadcast (ADS-B) is an aircraft tracking technology that relies on the global positioning system (GPS) and a datalink to broadcast (ADS-B Out) and receive (ADS-B In) data.

and should "own" the operational description, even where technology choices may be deferred to contractors. This topic is discussed further in Chapter 2.

An additional challenge is that considerable confusion on the part of non-FAA observers and stakeholders has resulted from ambiguous use of the NextGen label. At times, it has been used to mean the full, original JPDO vision; at other times, as a collective name for all the activities of the NextGen office, including basic modernization and replacement of existing facilities; and on occasion as a shorthand for "later than 2020." In the committee's view, NextGen, as currently instantiated, is a set of programs to implement a suite of incremental changes to the NAS. Although some technologies and/or systems will be new, in most cases, current plans call for them to be used in a way nearly identical to existing capabilities. NextGen's implementation plan employs a strategy that can be described as: "design a little, build a little, test a little, deploy a little." This aspect of the plan is understandable and reflects lessons learned from past efforts[10] as well as an industry-wide best practice of incremental change and development.

An important part of NextGen is addressing urgent requirements to replace aging equipment. Such modernization is essential and important, as the committee noted in its interim report.[11] NextGen also includes efforts to further deploy performance-based navigation, to redesign certain aspects of the airspace (such as rules and procedures and altitudes and headings), and to equip aircraft with technology (such as ADS-B) that can form the basis for future capabilities. NextGen has also come to encompass an additional broad range of activities expressed in various implementation plans, the NAS enterprise architecture, roadmaps, and calls for research, experimentation, and further incremental programs. Replacing or upgrading systems while the whole system must continuously and safely operate is an intricate undertaking, a process that the FAA seems to have mastered. These are complex systems that are undergoing constant change as aging equipment is replaced, as software is altered to improve resilience, and as operational requirements change. The successful operation of such systems requires ongoing alteration

---

[10] Such as the FAA's Advanced Automation System—a failed modernization effort begun in the 1980s that did not recognize the complexity associated with making major changes to software intensive national-scale systems. That effort resulted in significant delays and cost overruns, due in part to unrealistically ambitious goals without complete stakeholder agreement.

[11] National Research Council (NRC), *Interim Report of a Review of the Next Generation Air Transportation System Enterprise Architecture, Software, Safety, and Human Factors*, The National Academies Press, Washington, D.C., 2014.

and improvement, not just the occasional repair of faulty equipment and software.

NextGen is not, however, broadly transformational. That is, it does not set out a series of planned steps toward a fundamentally transformed end-state (such as free flight, decommissioning surveillance radar stations, automating air traffic control processes with a completely digital information infrastructure, or shifting authority from ground to air). And thus it is not an implementation of the early JPDO vision, which encompassed those ideas.[12] The executive order establishing the JPDO was entitled "Transformation of the National Air Transportation System,"[13] and early vision documents referred to ambitious goals such as integrated data streams for situational awareness in seamless multi-agency global operations, scalability, the use of emerging space-based communications and surveillance technologies.[14] Not all parts of original JPDO vision will be achieved in the foreseeable future. This was true even at the outset of NextGen and is understandable, given changes over time.[15] However, even the limited vision embraced at the start of NextGen has been reduced over time, while increasingly important challenges have not received adequate attention.[16] Many of the specific goals described in early JPDO discussions, such as free flight or air traffic control based on predefined 4-D flight trajectories, to enable global optimization of the airspace will not come to fruition in the foreseeable future. In fact, many of them will require significant research and experimentation before it can be known whether and in what form they are feasible. Unfortunately, over the course of the committee's work, it was clear that some stakeholders were still anticipating these capabilities from NextGen. Such goals await the now-distant full deployment of technical capabilities, the integration of these capabilities to support higher levels of automation and more distributed and autonomous operation, full equipage of virtually all aircraft with new components, and widespread revisions to procedures. More importantly, however, they will await the organizational will to

---

[12] Expressed in JPDO's "Concept of Operations for the Next Generation Air Transportation System," Version 3.2, 2011, http://www.dtic.mil/dtic/tr/fulltext/u2/a535795.pdf. See also Appendix B of the 2005 NRC report *Technology Pathways: Assessing the Integrated Plan for a Next Generation Air Transportation System* (The National Academies Press, Washington, D.C.) for an overview of JPDO objectives.

[13] White House, "Transformation of the National Air Transportation System," Executive Order, released November 18, 2008, http://georgewbush-whitehouse.archives.gov/news/releases/2008/11/20081118.html.

[14] See Appendix B of the 2005 NRC report *Technology Pathways* for an overview of JPDO objectives.

[15] For instance, the substantial future demand growth anticipated in early planning did not materialize.

[16] For instance, cybersecurity was not a significant concern in early JPDO planning.

modify the human roles and responsibilities of the participants in the NAS in order to meaningfully exploit the possibilities offered by these technologies.

A number of constraints may have plausibly contributed to the scaling back of NextGen ambitions, at least for the foreseeable future. These include the following:

- *Recognition that NextGen cannot fully remediate key NAS capacity limits.* Congestion in the NAS tends to be localized to certain regions, with more than one-half of activity in the approximately 20 so-called Metroplex sites, where the number of runways is a fundamental constraint on NAS throughput. Although there are opportunities to increase runway efficiency, such as some reduced separation, more parallel approaches, and so on, the realizable benefits of such are not yet clear. For example, wake vortex separation requirements may limit separation reduction, and local community resistance to noise and night flights may limit the introduction of new approach routes or extended hours that would increase the capacity of existing runways. In addition, new runways would be required to meet some capacity projections in certain locations.[17]
- *Uncertainty about future demand growth.* NAS capacity needs are hard to predict. Business dynamics, passenger demand and fuel costs are changing dramatically. The economic cycle in the 2000s weakened the capacity case for making wholesale changes in the NAS.
- *Impediments to the introduction of more automation, more distributed control, and significant changes to procedures.* Factors such as resistance (whether direct or due to cultural inertia) to significantly altering the nature of controller work, a conservative safety culture that makes changes to procedures slow and expensive, and limited resources and capacity to implement widespread changes to procedures have stalled efforts to make the fundamental changes to the concept of operations that the JPDO envisioned. It is difficult to distinguish specifically how much each of these factors contributes, but it will be critical to address these organizational and cultural factors if full advantage is to be taken of new technological possibilities.[18]

---

[17] See, for example, Transportation Research Board, *Airport Cooperative Research Program: Evaluating Airfield Capacity*, 2012, http://onlinepubs.trb.org/onlinepubs/acrp/acrp_rpt_079.pdf, and FAA, *FACT3: Airport Capacity Needs in the National Airspace System*, 2015, http://www.faa.gov/airports/planning_capacity/media/FACT3-Airport-Capacity-Needs-in-the-NAS.pdf.

[18] The 2014 NRC report *Autonomy Research for Civil Aviation: Toward a New Era of Flight* (The National Academies Press, Washington, D.C.) explores increasingly autonomous systems and their implications for civil aviation.

In short, NextGen will not provide a means to, say, double air traffic capacity by 2025,[19] nor does it offer a way to address increasingly urgent requirements for strengthened security, greater robustness, and evolvability to meet new challenges, such as addressing projected unmanned aircraft systems (UAS) traffic. NextGen is also not currently expected to significantly change roles in place today (e.g., giving pilots more authority). While many readers of this report will find these assertions obviously true, during its investigations, the committee heard references to and vestiges of these ambitious goals. It is appropriate for NextGen goals and aims to have changed over time, and in some cases there were ambitions informally affiliated with NextGen that were not actually ever part of the NextGen effort. That being the case, it seems appropriate for the FAA, working with stakeholders, to clearly circumscribe these goals and ambitions and to clearly articulate the program's actual current goals and ambitions.

With only modest changes to the operation of the NAS through 2018, NextGen programs are better described as a technology-refresh effort rather than the transformational activity envisioned by JPDO. This understanding does not undermine the critical importance of NextGen, because its programs will replace and modernize critical components of the NAS that would otherwise become increasingly difficult and expensive to maintain as a result of age. Thus the bulk of the currently pursued programs labeled as "NextGen" are properly thought of as a necessary and inevitable upgrade to existing technology, supporting essentially unmodified operating practices. Nevertheless, there are things that can be done now to help ease the path toward eventual significant change. For instance, a few of the NextGen programs introduce technologies that, if properly embraced by a future-oriented system architecture, could form the basis for transformation and pave the way toward more ambitious goals. New technologies such as ADS-B and digital communication are important digital infrastructure for future enhancements, but their potential is masked by other impediments, such as those cited above.

The committee's conclusion that NextGen today is primarily an incremental modernization effort should not suggest that NextGen, therefore, has an obvious completed state. Given the continuing rapid pace of technological evolution and ongoing changes in what is demanded of the NAS (see Chapter 4 for a discussion of UAS and cybersecurity as examples),

---

[19] Early planning documents used to motivate NextGen noted that some models projected that the number of passengers could more than double by 2025 (see, for example, Gisele Mohler, FAA, "Airport Capacity Planning and NextGen," presentation to the Eastern Region Airport Conference, March 2008, http://www.faa.gov/airports/eastern/airports_news_events/hershey/media_08/Mohler-Eastern%20Region%20Arpt%20Conf08%20-GM.pdf ).

the NextGen effort is properly seen as an ongoing process, punctuated by particular efforts focused on particular capabilities. Such an effort will require an appropriate systems architecture (discussed in Chapter 2) and a risk-managed development process (discussed in Chapter 4).

Much has changed even in the course of the committee's work, including the appointment of a new assistant administrator for NextGen. In a recent report to Congress, the FAA has presented a more realistic indication of what NextGen is relative to what it was envisioned (i.e., how far it has been scaled back).[20] The committee urges that a clear realignment of expectations for all parties take place. Revised expectations should not only concern what the future state of the NAS will be, but also reflect the kind of evolvability that needs to be built into the system so that later technologies (which may either come along or be modifications of planned technologies), new requirements, and changing market conditions can be exploited. Resetting expectations with a clear baseline will provide a useful foundation on which to build.

**Finding: Stakeholder expectations for NextGen have become misaligned with current planning as NextGen, and its constituent programs have changed over time. This misalignment causes challenges both for the FAA and for stakeholders.**

**Finding: Although technological and procedural improvements have been introduced into the NAS, elements of the NAS rely on outdated technology, and the system has not been significantly changed to take advantage of available information and communications technologies or to enable major improvements in how the airspace can be organized and managed. "NextGen" has become a misnomer.**

**Finding: Modernization is critical. Although not the transformation originally envisioned for NextGen, refreshing already extant capabilities with improved and more reliable technology is necessary, and support for a major push to modernize is needed.**

**Recommendation: The Federal Aviation Administration (FAA), Congress, and all National Airspace System stakeholders should reset expectations for the Next Generation Air Transportation System. The FAA should explicitly qualify the early transformational vision in a way that clearly articulates the new realities.**

---

[20] FAA, *NextGen Priorities Joint Implementation Plan: Executive Report to Congress*, October 2014, http://www.faa.gov/nextgen/media/ng_priorities.pdf.

# 2

# Assert Architectural Leadership

A key part of the committee's initial focus was on the enterprise architecture of Next Generation Air Transportation System (NextGen), per its tasking. What soon became clear, however, was that an enterprise architecture[1] is a necessary but not sufficient component of a successful "system of systems,"[2] such as NextGen. An *enterprise architecture* serves as documentation and support of existing systems and business processes. A *system architecture* models and defines the structure and behavior of a system in a way that supports reasoning about the system and its characteristics. See Box 2.1 for more on the distinction between enterprise architecture and system architecture. Accordingly, and consistent with other elements of its task, such as software development,[3] the committee

---

[1] The Office of Management and Budget (OMB) requires that every federal agency have an enterprise architecture designed to "promote mission success by serving as an authoritative reference, and by promoting functional integration and resource optimization with both internal and external service partners" (OMB, "The Common Approach to Federal Enterprise Architecture," Washington, D.C., May 2, 2012, http://www.whitehouse.gov/sites/default/files/omb/assets/egov_docs/common_approach_to_federal_ea.pdf, p. 5). Generally, an enterprise architecture (and its associated legislation and treatment by OMB) targets traditional "enterprise" information technology systems and are not focused on systems-of systems that include real-time control, operations, and so on.

[2] For simplicity, the committee will usually use the term "system," because all systems of systems are systems themselves.

[3] The legislation referencing the committee's task (P.L. 112-95, Section 212) uses the term "software development," which is sometimes understood narrowly by laypeople as referring to such things as coding techniques or software development methodology. Here,

explored the question of architecture more broadly, focusing also on the system architecture for NextGen.

The committee has drawn on its collective experience and expertise (in software engineering, as executives at major government contractors, and in the architecture of large-scale systems) to develop its recommendations, which are focused around the importance and implications of system architecture. It is reasonable to hope that there might be architectures in other domains, at companies or in other agencies, that would serve as useful exemplars. However, it is difficult to point to specific other architectures as exemplars without having conducted an in-depth analysis of them, an effort that would have gone beyond the time and resources available for this study. Moreover, NextGen and the National Airspace System (NAS) pose distinctive challenges, and the committee notes that pointing to any one specific other example would be a distraction, as it would too readily raise the possibility of arguments about whether or not the comparison is fair, or about ways in which the analogy or comparison does not work. Instead, this chapter focuses on the features and aspects needed in a system architecture for a system such as NextGen and points out lessons to be learned from industrial approaches to architectural governance and the development of architectural leadership. This chapter discusses the committee's assessment of the Federal Aviation Administration's (FAA's) current architectural approach for NextGen, key elements of architectural leadership, and recommendations for change.

## FAA'S CURRENT APPROACH TO ARCHITECTURE

During the course of its study, the committee heard briefings and studied documents related to the FAA's NAS enterprise architecture and its overall approach to system architecture. This section provides the committee's impressions regarding what the FAA is currently doing (at the time of the committee's information gathering) with respect to architecture, and the next sections offer recommendations for how the FAA could improve its approach.

---

too, the committee has taken a broader view more consistent with contemporary software engineering theory and practice that, especially in the case of large-scale complex systems, the term encompasses such pre-coding activities as requirements specification, system architecture, and design as well as coding and testing. As with its use of the term system architecture, this broad notion of the term software development ensures that the full range of software issues critical to NextGen success are considered. NextGen contains a large software element, and that software element will have an architecture (and should have its own architecture description). Standard practice in software architecture recognizes that the "development view," the structure of the code being developed, is just one view. Many of the important attributes about which one would want to reason are defined only by moving outside the development view to a run-time, data, or other view.

> **BOX 2.1 An Enterprise Architecture Is
> Necessary but Not Sufficient**
>
> Every system has an architecture, even when that architecture is not documented. Just as building architects distinguish architectures (what they have in mind) from blueprints (how their ideas are recorded), current practice in architecting distinguishes architectures from the artifacts, documents, models, or other work products expressing those architectures. Mature architecting practices include making "tacit architectures" explicit by means of architecture descriptions. Typically, these are distinguished as follows:[1]
>
> - *Architecture (of a system)*: fundamental concepts or properties of a system in its environment embodied in its elements, relationships, and in the principles of its design and evolution.
> - *Architecture description*: work product used to express an architecture.
>
> The maturation of architecting as a discipline has had to contend with a variety of distinctions, such as distinguishing an enterprise architecture from a systems architecture and from a software architecture. Each of these as typically understood has strengths and weaknesses:
>
> - *Enterprise architecture* has evolved out of the management of large information technology (IT) systems. Some versions of enterprise architecture are little more than "bookkeeping" of IT assets. Other versions have come to focus on critical but "softer" aspects of enterprises, such as business vision, strategy and goals, human resources, and organizations.
> - *System architecture* is perhaps the most mature of the three in its management of "non-functional" concerns such as reliability, affordability, and safety.

Although the FAA noted in briefings that the NAS enterprise architecture is meant to serve multiple purposes ("to align systems and technologies, identify duplication of effort, address the need for increased efficiency and interoperability, provide a common language for linkages and communications, and provide a framework for managing change by facilitating efficient identification of changes and implementations"), it was described to the committee as an explanatory set of documents, which is insufficient to meet NAS and NextGen needs (see Box 2.1). The enterprise architecture "describes the enterprise that directly supports operational air traffic services" and "describes the enterprise that supports FAA administrative operations."[4] Parts of the enterprise architecture

---

[4] Remarks from FAA briefing "Role of Enterprise Architecture NextGen: Briefing to National Research Council" to study committee, March 2013.

> - *Software architecture* is perhaps the most mature in its modeling practices and associated automated tools.
>
> The current state of enterprise architecture is not adequately mature to manage large, distributed, real-time systems where safety-critical concerns predominate nor is it clear that even the best instantiation of an enterprise architecture is intended for such uses. Enterprise architecture has focused on "bookkeeping" of enterprise IT assets. For a system such as NextGen, a more comprehensive notion of architecture is needed. Having high-quality descriptions of a system is insufficient to ensure that the depicted system is fit for anything. Standard ISO/IEC/IEEE 42010$^2$ addresses this dichotomy. The quality of the design choices have to be assessed on their own, and the quality of the drawings is not a surrogate.
>
> An enterprise architecture is typically interpreted as a set of documents instead of a set of decisions. This is consistent with what the committee learned in its briefings. However, an emphasis on documents and compliance over decision making is misplaced. A close reading of architecture description standards, such as the Department of Defense Architecture Framework, will show that this issue was recognized by the description standard authors. Such frameworks are careful to identify the need for an architecture team to identify the purpose of the system, the purpose of the architecture, the information needed, and only then fold that information into standardized document products. That basic discipline should be employed in any assessment of an architecture. The linkage between architecture purpose, stakeholder concerns, and the contents of a description document is explicit in Standard 42010. In this report, the committee calls for that broader approach and calls it a "system architecture."
>
> ---
> [1] ISO/IEC/IEEE 42010:2011, 2011.
> [2] Ibid.

are used to justify expenditures; an enterprise architecture is required as programs work through the acquisition management system (AMS) and must be approved by the FAA's Joint Resource Council. The enterprise architecture also serves to meet the OMB requirement for agency-wide enterprise architecture as laid out in the Clinger-Cohen Act.[5] Given that a goal of the act is to ensure efficient capital planning and investment in information technology (IT), the enterprise architecture's focus on business structures and process is not surprising. In briefings, when asked to discuss the system architecture, FAA staff noted that there is no "software

---
[5] The Information Technology Management Reform Act (ITMRA) (Division E) and the Federal Acquisition Reform Act (FARA) (Division D) were signed into law as part of the National Defense Authorization Act for Fiscal Year 1996. The ITMRA and FARA were subsequently designated the Clinger Cohen Act of 1996 (P.L.104-106), encompassing both.

or hardware architecture" per se for NextGen and the NAS as a whole but that enterprise architecture at the program level describes how the system (comprised of software and hardware) will work.[6]

The FAA uses an integrated systems engineering framework (NAS ISEF)[7] to build their enterprise architecture, which is based loosely on the Department of Defense architecture framework (DoDAF).[8] According to briefings provided to the committee, program offices develop their own architectures, in compliance with the NAS ISEF and in compliance with high-level interface specifications embodied in additional diagrams contained within the enterprise architecture. Additionally, the Chief Architect's office ensures that the enterprise architecture is integrated horizontally (identifying linkages and interdependencies from system to system within the system-of-systems) and vertically within functions or components (to address shortfalls and help facilitate prioritization analysis).

The NAS ISEF supports visualizing the broad scope and complexities of the architecture and allows for varying views. These views provide overviews and details aimed at specific stakeholders. In addition to the views provided by DoDAF—all view, systems view, operational view, and technical view—the NextGen enterprise architecture provides for two additional views that are important for acquisition. The executive view provides planning roadmaps and highlights the evolution and delivery of NAS capabilities, and the financial view provides expenditure forecasts. While these multiple views provide overviews and details aimed at the varying levels of the NAS, there is a risk that each program office will see only what it needs to (in a narrow sense) without an understanding of the full picture and without ensuring that the various perspectives in the architecture are consistent and interoperable. Further, the absence of a system architecture for the entirety of NextGen makes it difficult for the developers of the individual subsystems and components to reason about the impact that the characteristics of their separate systems will have on such key overall NextGen system characteristics as safety, security, efficiency, robustness, and evolvability.

---

[6] The FAA is in the process of buying the hardware and software that comprises NextGen, and each component will be, in fact, a system in its own right. It will then have an architecture, whether or not the FAA has chosen to make it explicit and effective. For instance, both ERAM and STARS/TAMR pre-date NextGen and will need to be adapted to the NextGen architecture. As noted in NRC-AF-2008, the quality of the decomposition is likely to be a major determinant of success. If the hardware and software architectures have not been considered, then there is only chance to rely on for the quality of the decomposition.

[7] Details about this framework are available at Federal Aviation Administration (FAA), "Publications," https://nasea.faa.gov/publications/main (accessed April 7, 2015).

[8] Details about the DoDAF are available at Department of Defense, Chief Information +Officer, "The DoDAF Architecture Framework Version 2.02, Change 1," released January 2015, http://dodcio.defense.gov/TodayinCIO/DoDArchitectureFramework.aspx.

Ultimately, the committee's conclusion with regard to the NAS enterprise architecture is that the as-is architecture has evolved to also become the dominant understanding of the to-be architecture. That is, the existing design and deployment of the NAS embodies a tacit architecture that is described, at a non-detailed level, by the NAS enterprise architecture documentation. This induced, system-of-system architecture is, therefore, bottom-up and program-driven, and imposes implicit limits on what (and how) system capabilities can be realized. This has ramifications for how effective it can be, especially for reasoning about safety, security, and robustness, and in laying groundwork for future evolvability and enhancements.

As described in the committee's interim report,[9] the FAA developed an enterprise architecture responsive to OMB's requirements. The committee was concerned that there was insufficient technical content in the enterprise architecture to allow clear traceability to lower-level architecture. As first defined by the Institute of Electrical and Electronics Engineers in Standard 1471,[10] a system architecture is "the fundamental organization of a system embodied in its components, their relationships to each other and to the environment and the principles guiding its design and evolution." (Box 2.2 describes system architecture in more detail.)

Although the documentation regarding the enterprise architecture is extensive, as noted above, the de facto "system architecture" for the NAS is the unmodified system as it is today, regardless of any documents to the contrary. The current enterprise architecture appears to be a set of functional enclaves that are providing individual services, described in a set of documents at the NAS enterprise architecture level. Additional improvements and modifications seem to be either changes to what is already deployed, or overlays onto what is already there. Discerning precisely what FAA's architectural approach and strategy is was challenging, and some of it had to be inferred. The documents for the as-is architecture that the committee reviewed do not use abstraction to higher-level concepts that are used in the mid-term and far-term document sets. (For example, one cannot trace an ADS-B target from the ADS-B receiver to a display screen without going through several programs' documentation.) Nor is it clear that the abstractions generated are sufficient to describe the

---

[9] National Research Council (NRC), *Interim Report of a Review of the Next Generation Air Transportation System Enterprise Architecture, Software, Safety, and Human Factors*, The National Academies Press, Washington, D.C., 2014.

[10] Institute of Electrical and Electronics Engineers (IEEE) Standard 1471:2000 has since been retired and replaced by the revised standard, ISO/IEC/IEEE 42010:2011, "Systems and Software Engineering—Architecture Description" (International Organization for Standardization (ISO)/International Electrotechnical Commission (IEC)/IEEE, December 2011, http://www.iso.org/iso/catalogue_detail.htm?csnumber=50508).

## BOX 2.2 On System Architecture

The 2010 National Research Council report *Critical Code: Software Producibility for Defense* offers a useful description of architecture and its importance:[1]

> Just as in physical systems, architectural commitments comprise more than structural connections among components of a system. The commitments also encompass decisions regarding the principal domain abstractions to be represented in the software and how they will be represented and acted upon. The commitments also include expectations regarding performance, security, and other behavioral characteristics of the constituent components of a system, such that an overall architectural model can facilitate prediction of significant quality-related characteristics of a system that is consistent with the architectural model. Architecture represents the earliest and often most important design decisions—those that are the hardest to change and the most critical to get right. Architecture makes it possible to structure requirements based on an understanding of what is actually possible from an engineering standpoint—and what is infeasible in the present state of technology. It provides a mechanism for communications among the stakeholders, including the infrastructure providers, and managers of other systems with requirements for interoperation. It is also the first design artifact that addresses the so-called non-functional attributes, such as performance, modifiability, reliability, and security that in turn drive the ultimate quality and capability of the system. Architecture is an important enabler of reuse and the key to system evolution, enabling management of future uncertainty. In this regard, architecture is the primary determiner of modularity and thus the nature and degree to which multiple design decisions can be decoupled from each other. Thus, when there are areas of likely or potential change, whether it be in system functionality, performance, infrastructure, or other areas, architecture decisions can be made to encapsulate them and so increase the extent to which the overall engineering activity is insulated from the uncertainties associated with these localized changes.

A principal goal of a system architecture is to provide a specification of the structure of the system in order to foster the design and implementation of a system whose important properties are sufficiently well understood, able to be reasoned about, and assured.[2] The architecture must provide a high-level view of the general nature of the system and support an understanding of the lower levels of the system that are needed in order to be assured that the system will satisfy key properties and behaviors. A well-formed architecture should provide a clear and consistent view of how each of its levels relates to the other levels and how the components of each of the various levels fit with each other. Key mechanisms for doing this are hierarchy, abstraction, and separation of concerns. A hierarchical architecture specifies how each component is comprised of a collection of lower-level components. Abstraction expresses functions of higher-level components of the hierarchy in terms of general concepts that suppress the details of the lower-level components. Abstraction allows for hiding specifics of decisions so that only the properties of concern need be addressed, avoiding inappropriate complexity. Separation of concerns helps ensure that appropriate decomposition takes place and reduces the opportunity for confusing overlaps or mismatches across components and views. The specifications, at all levels, are used to reason about properties the system must ensure.

A higher-level component specification is essentially a summary of the key features, aspects, and behaviors that the component must implement. Typically these are specified as the set of interfaces that the component presents to the other components at its architectural level. But this specification should not address how these features and behaviors are to be achieved, except when dominating, systemic concerns prevail (for example, to specify canonical information sources for certain sorts of functions). Specifications of how to satisfy the specification are abstracted away at the higher level in order to provide flexibility and evolvability to implementers, thereby enabling changes to the actual implementation as system contexts, requirements, and experience change over time. The component's decomposition into lower-level subcomponents provides these implementation details, specifying how the mandated abstract features and behaviors are to be realized. The features and behaviors of these lower-level components are specified, in turn, as sets of interfaces to each other that are abstractions of still lower-level subcomponents. Ultimately, a hierarchical architecture specification's decomposition stops at a set of leaf components, namely, the lowest-level components whose structure need not be further elaborated in order to reason about the system architecture.

A hierarchical system architecture can be useful even if its specifications are relatively informal, as may well be the case early in the conceptualization and initial development of a complex system, or in the case of a system about which relatively few assurances are needed. In these cases, the architectural specification may need to be only lightly decomposed, and left relatively informal, with most of the development work being left to subsequent designers and implementers. If the architecture's leaf components specify only very-high-level features and capabilities, then a very great deal must be assumed about the correctness of the implementation of these subcomponents, and there is consequent room for relatively greater doubt about whether the eventually implemented system will satisfy its critical properties and characteristics.

For complex systems, about which there need to be strong assurances about many potentially conflicting characteristics, more highly elaborated and more detailed architectural specifications are important. Such system architectures will probably start out as relatively informal high-level specifications, but should be expected to become increasingly complete and precise over time, as requirements, contexts, and available technologies all become better understood.[3] The importance of more complete and precise architecture specifications is that they become increasingly effective in supporting increasingly definitive reasoning about key characteristics of the overall system. Eventually, the system architecture should be decomposed to sufficiently low levels, in sufficient detail and with sufficient precision, to support needed reasoning about such key overall system characteristics as safety, security, speed, robustness, and evolvability.[4]

At present, the NextGen system architecture appears to be tacit or at best, still at a very high level and largely specified quite informally. While this might be an acceptable, indeed inevitable, state of affairs early in the development of such a complex and critical system, it poses considerable risk and difficulty at this relatively late stage in the development of NextGen. The lack of a well-defined, sufficiently deeply decomposed system architecture for NextGen poses at least two serious problems. First, the fact that the architecture description is insufficiently deeply defined means that the specifications for the system's component parts

*continued*

> **BOX 2.2 Continued**
>
> may be too vague and incomplete to provide effective guidance to the developers of these lowest-level components. Unfortunately, if firm assurances about security and robustness (for example) of the overall system are required, then correct implementation of these vaguely specified components will have to be assumed. The more vague and incomplete these specifications, the greater the risk that their implementations may not be correct, leaving assurance of the desired properties in doubt. Second, even if an architecture specification does indeed decompose down to lower-level subcomponents, it is still essential that the interfaces to these components be very carefully specified. Imprecise specifications make it difficult to assure that the delivered components will indeed fit with each other as needed. More important, however, the less precisely the specifications of the components and their interfaces are specified, the less definitively the critical properties of the overall system can be determined.
>
> Finally, a system architecture may encompass separate, but related, sub-architecture (sometimes referred to as architecture views), each of which addresses a different set of issues. Thus, for example, a system architecture may well incorporate a data architecture, specifying how data is managed; a user interface architecture, specifying how various system capabilities are presented to users; a safety architecture, specifying how various safety risks are attenuated by the system; a resilience architecture, specifying how the system can operate even though some components have failed; and a security architecture, specifying how the system provides safeguards against possible damage due to attacks. Each of these needs to be complementary to the overall system architecture and be consistent with each other—in other words, both horizontal and vertical correspondences are needed. And for each of these architectures, it is important that each component be described in terms of the abstract features and capabilities that must be provided, and that implementation details not be provided. A data architecture, for example, might specify that certain types of data must be logically centralized, leaving to the elaboration of this specification details and decisions about whether the data should or should not be physically centralized.

complete system. Moreover, it is not clear how or if there are systems engineering work products that are derived from the midterm architecture.

As one example, the committee noted that the first architecture rule written in the AV-1 "Mid-Term Overview and Summary Information" document states that

> NAS [enterprise architecture] products shall be developed and decomposed only to the level of detail required to portray enterprise "To-Be" Operational Improvements/Sustainment and transformation priorities. The level of detail should articulate enterprise-level operations, functions, and systems without infringing on Program-level detail. Thus, the lowest

> Note that the need for a coordinated collection of different subarchitectures is necessary even for systems and products that are far less complex and far better understood than NextGen. Thus, as an analogy, a building architect will typically have considerable experience in building office buildings and a firm grasp on the characteristics of materials and structures. Even so, each new office building project must start with a building architecture that must be rigorous, complete, and sufficiently precise about electrical systems, plumbing systems, elevator systems, and heating/cooling systems, in addition to the configuration of the building's various structural members. The need for analogously complete subarchitectures is even more critical in the case of NextGen, which is an interconnected system of systems with far more complexity than an office building. With regard to data alone, NextGen has to cope with a range of information from weather data to flight plans to real-time traffic data to emergency declarations. In both cases, the building architecture and the NextGen system architecture, different notations and formalisms may be used to support specification of the different kinds of architectural features. But each notation or formalism must be precise, and the specification must be sufficiently deeply decomposed, in order to support reasoning about that architectural feature and its relations to the other architectural features.
>
> ---
>
> [1] NRC, *Critical Code: Software Producibility for Defense*, The National Academies Press, Washington, D.C., 2010, pp. 68-69.
>
> [2] *Architecting* is the process of conceiving, defining, expressing, documenting, communicating, certifying proper implementation of, maintaining, and improving an architecture throughout a system's life cycle, per ISO/IEC/IEEE 42010:2011, (2011, pp. 1-46).
>
> [3] A note on precision: precision in this discussion should not be viewed as an absolute, rather, precision evolves with the understanding of engineering trade-offs between requirements, designs, and business constraints throughout the life cycle.
>
> [4] If very firm assurances about these characteristics are required, then the architecture eventually must be defined in a notation that is sufficiently formal and precise to support the definitive reasoning needed for such assurances.

level of detail (e.g., leaf nodes) of the enterprise-level products should serve as the context/highest level of Program-level architecture elements.[11]

Although the infrastructure set up by the FAA to host its enterprise architecture is robust, there seems to be no explicit connection between

---

[11] FAA, "Mid-Term Overview and Summary Information (AV-1), Version 3.0, Part of Integrated Mid-Term Release Package 3.0," document NAS-EA-AV-1-Mid-Term-v3.0-022814, National Airspace System Enterprise Architecture, Office of NextGen, February 28, 2014, https://nasea.faa.gov/architecture/enterprise/display/4/tab/Mid-Term, p. 4. This document has been superseded by Version 4.0, in which similar language can be found on p. 12.

the "leaf nodes" and the program-level architectures or descriptive documents. This may be sufficient to meet the OMB mandate for an enterprise architecture and to rationalize acquisition efforts, but it is insufficient to support the technical steering of an effective system architecture. Capturing and providing appropriately detailed abstract specifications and interfaces is essential to the ability to reason about NextGen's key properties and improves the ability to determine where and how to make improvements and how to assess impacts on other subsystems.

NextGen goals and associated programs should, by definition, provoke changes and adjustments in the NAS system architecture. That tacit architecture is diffused through many different programs, not all of which are under NextGen control. NextGen's programs have developed, not under the control of the NextGen office, but under other FAA organizations. Thus, one program's engineers must exhaustively search through all other programs' documentation—hoping that it is up to date—to assess and understand changes. In such a situation, engineers may be unable to gain sufficiently clear insights into the nature of needed subsystems and subcomponents to assure that the program's product will integrate correctly with the other subsystems and make the needed contributions to required system-level requirements.

The committee urges a focus on system architecture that reflects a set of fundamental, structural decisions about a system and that is distinguished from the architecture description, a document that records those decisions (much like the FAA uses the enterprise architecture). The FAA needs a system architecture for the NAS so as to ensure proper operation of the system; allow proper analyses for prediction of system behavior, performance, security, safety, and so on; and ensure future flexibility. A proper system architecture specifies the interfaces between different subsystems sufficiently enough that their design and implementation can proceed independently with reasonable confidence that they will interoperate correctly. (Internet protocols are a textbook example of this.) The current situation relates to the basic contract mechanism used by the FAA. Different functional elements are being built by different contractors selected and managed by different programs that may not have a clear view of the system architecture.

However, certain basic services need to be provided to various higher-level services as abstractions where the basic services are implemented system wide. Examples include security properties to assure that NextGen is resistant to possible attacks, robustness properties to assure that the system will degrade gracefully in the presence of equipment failures and unexpected contingencies, and evolvability properties to assure that NextGen can be modified and enhanced as new challenges are presented and so the advantages of new technologies can be exploited. Abstraction should allow design decisions such as physical locations, formats of data, protocols, and so on to be hidden until the specifics of those decisions are needed. An appropriate separation of concerns can ensure that adequate information is available for reasoning about systemic properties.

Data that is crucial to the various services needs be defined carefully by an abstraction that is common to all services and that provides site-independent guarantees on availability, timeliness, ordering, throughput of the data, and so on. For example, various high-level functions need to be able to store their specific data, but there are important guarantees that the high-level functions need about data storage. To achieve this effectively, there would need to be a customizable data service structure that can be tailored by each high-level service according to its needs but which guarantees properties such as availability. Similarly, high-level functions need to have guarantees that when errors arise (for whatever reason) there are alternatives for backup data storage, processing, database availability, and so on.[12] Without such abstractions and associated interfaces, developers of higher-level functions would begin to implement such elements individually, which is happening, as the committee learned through briefings with both the FAA and contractors. Although this is understandable given the current context, it is unlikely to be a very satisfactory approach for the system as a whole.[13] Additional data properties, such as ownership, span of use, demand, safety, security, latency, freshness, and location, often have architectural significance and need to be managed at the architectural level. Moreover, different categories of data may necessitate services with very different characteristics.

As an example of a system-wide service in NextGen, the Surveillance and Broadcast Services (SBS) Final System Specification Rev. 4 states that

> SBS is a system of systems, requiring functionality on participating aircraft and vehicles, in a ground infrastructure, and in participating automation systems. The SBS System provides ADS-B, TIS-B, ADS-R, Wide Area Multilateration (WAM), Airport Surface Surveillance Capability (ASSC), FIS-B, VHF Voice Communications, and Weather Observation Services. *Performance for each of the services is specified and allocated herein*

---

[12] Modern industrial approaches such as Oracle, SQL Server, or Google's Spanner are examples of the provision of this sort of functionality.

[13] And indeed, inconsistencies or misunderstandings related to data definitions often lead to interface errors among software components. A stark example of this sort of error resulted in the loss of the Mars Orbiter in the late 1990s when NASA used the metric system and its contractor used English units of measurement. Modern software architecture standards all call for a "data view" or "logical view" or something equivalent. This is usually conceived of as an implementation-independent definition of core data, which is transformed into physical data models during implementation.

to the aircraft, surface vehicles, the ground infrastructure, and the ATC automation system. [emphasis added][14]

This statement suggests that the NextGen organization provides little architectural direction to the enterprise. Although the choice above may in the end be a plausible architectural decision, the committee is concerned that this choice is being made by default rather than the result of a considered process through trades on the bases of explicitly stated criteria.[15] Moreover, insufficient abstractions to high-level services place roadblocks in the way of those attempting to insert new technologies or services (such as unmanned aircraft systems (UAS) or cybersecurity protections, discussed in Chapter 3) into the context of the NAS.

As noted above, the FAA has adopted the DoDAF in an attempt to satisfy both OMB's requirements as well as the need for a system architecture required to develop its NextGen systems. Reinforcing the committee's conclusion that the enterprise architecture, as currently used and understood, falls short in providing what a proper system architecture could provide, a recent Department of Transportation Inspector General's assessment of the enterprise architecture shows the FAA falling short in the OMB sense:

> Overall, the [enterprise architecture]'s usefulness as a strategic planning tool for NextGen has been limited due to incomplete information, a lack of policy and guidance, and unresolved NextGen design decisions.[16]

That the system architecture is not well developed is hard to discern for two reasons: (1) the nearly exclusive focus on the enterprise architecture, which is important but does not address the technical issues of just how a new NAS could be built and (2) the NAS system architecture could be shown to meet all of the new requirements that have been communicated to the Congress and the public. A complex system (of systems) requires several architecture perspectives, each aimed at demonstrating how each of several different kinds of requirements are to be met. Each perspective needs to be clearly communicated so that developers can understand the local intentions and system integrators can reason

---

[14] FAA, "Final Program Requirements, SBS-002, Revision 04," Surveillance and Broadcast Services Program Office, June 26, 2012, p. 22. See Appendix C for acronyms.

[15] This is recommended in NRC, *Pre-Milestone A and Early-Phase Systems Engineering* (The National Academies Press, Washington, D.C.), a 2008 report that examines the role systems engineering can play in the acquisition lifecycle.

[16] Department of Transportation, *Addressing Underlying Causes for NextGen Delays Will Require Sustained FAA Leadership and Action*, Office of Inspector General Audit Report AV-2014-031, February 25, 2014, https://www.oig.dot.gov/library-item/28823.

about system behaviors and unintended consequences. Indeed, one of the main roles of a system architecture is to facilitate the ability to envision and express how the system will (or could) evolve. It can reveal how new capabilities (e.g., ADS-B surveillance) fit in and what implications they have. A system architecture allows one component's evolution to be planned to co-evolve with other components, and so on. Rather than being a simple snapshot or a log of changes to date, a well-developed system architecture should play a critical role in system evolution over time, providing a way to look forward and map out likely outcomes from a variety of scenarios.

A useful reference with which to examine architectural approaches is the 2008 NRC report *Pre-Milestone A and Early-Phase Systems Engineering*.[17] Although that report's recommendations do not universally apply to the FAA's situation, they are nonetheless useful. In particular, the 2008 report identifies certain patterns indicative of success and failure, including the need for appropriate engineering talent and clear lines of authority, the need to perform trade-offs and manage complexity early in the process, the importance of a stable set of system requirements, and the need to plan ahead for change through architectural choices. As discussed in the rest of this report, the committee observes some of these success patterns being ignored in NextGen.

The upshot of the limitations in the existing enterprise architecture discussed above is that programmatic risk and engineering risk are both increased. In addition, architectural perspectives have not been exposed to users (pilots and controllers) at sufficient depth and with sufficient interaction and discussion about how operations would change as a result of implementing new features (which themselves are not documented at a depth sufficient to foster useful conversations). Furthermore, it will be much more difficult to evolve the system to meet requirements and take advantage of new technologies.

See Box 2.3 for a discussion of an ERAM system failure[18] that occurred during the course of the committee's work; the committee's analysis of this failure reinforces the importance and potential of more comprehensive approaches to system architecture. This incident and subsequent analysis are suggestive of the need for proper system architectures that would allow modeling and reasoning about the system as a whole. ERAM was developed as a replacement for the legacy host system; it provides core functionality to the NAS. This may have seemed initially like a component for component replacement. But ERAM relies on complex

---

[17] NRC, *Pre-Milestone A and Early-Phase Systems Engineering*, 2008.
[18] The fire at Chicago Air Route Traffic Control Center in September 2014 provides further evidence of an architectural resilience failure in the NAS architecture.

## BOX 2.3 April 2014 En Route Automation Modernization Failure and Architectural Implications

During the course of the committee's work, the Los Angeles En-Route Air Traffic Control Center (ZLA ARTCC) experienced failures of the En Route Automation Modernization (ERAM) Flight Data Manager (FDM) software resulting in a ground stop for all flights passing through that center. FAA statements at the time summarized the situation:

> On April 30, 2014, an FAA air traffic system that processes flight plan information experienced problems while processing a flight plan filed for a U-2 aircraft that operates at very high altitudes under visual flight rules. [...] The computer system interpreted the flight as a more typical low altitude operation, and began processing it for a route below 10,000 feet. The extensive number of routings that would have been required to de-conflict the aircraft with lower-altitude flights used a large amount of available memory and interrupted the computer's other flight-processing functions.[1]

Because ERAM is a major NextGen program, the committee asked for information about this failure in order to better understand how such failures come about, how they are handled, and what improvements with regard to architecture and software development the committee could suggest.[2] While not tasked with undertaking a complete analysis of this or any other specific incident, the committee offers the following limited analysis—based on necessarily limited data—of why such failures are a concern and how appropriate system architecture and software development approaches could help reduce the likelihood of such failures in the future.

First, it should be noted that this incident led to a considerable loss of air traffic control service. The result could have been catastrophic. That it was not catastrophic does not mitigate the seriousness of the event. In the committee's view, the investigation of this (or similar events affecting so much of the NAS) and the subsequent reporting should have been at the same scale as would have been required had there been an accident with loss of life.

The documentation and reporting suggests that ERAM failed essentially in its entirety (including its backup system), and that indicates a serious, systemic design flaw. Incorrect flight data was entered for a particular aircraft that, coupled with the activity of the aircraft in question, resulted in exhaustion of a fixed-size memory area, which ultimately led to a failure of the flight data processor. The backup system suffered from the same bad data. There were several ways in which this failure exposed poor design choices:

- *Failure due to exhaustion of resources.* The system should be monitoring resources, data integrity, equipment availability, response times, queue lengths, activity levels, and many other system parameters continuously. Provision for handling deviations from planned levels should be present for all system parameters.
- *Unhandled software exceptions in a critical system.* There was apparently an unhandled software exception that led to the exhaustion of resources.
- *Mishandling of poor data entry.* Apparently, the altitude of the aircraft in question was entered incorrectly. The very large extent of the consequent adjustments to civil air traffic flight plans could have triggered a resiliency response (such

as an "Are you sure?" reply to the flight plan as entered). Financial services sites routinely do this, for example, when amounts entered for online transactions are outside of determined normative bounds. This is all part of a properly designed input-validation (and taint removal) process.

- *Primary and backup systems failed simultaneously.* The simultaneous failure of primary and backup systems is a design flaw resulting in part from an inadequately considered system architecture. The decision to automatically hand something off to a backup computer is appropriate for a hardware failure; it is also likely acceptable when the failure is caused by the total state of the system. In this case, though, the flaw was in how one specific input in combination with a particular aircraft's behavior was handled. The system was always going to fail with these bad inputs. Handling such a failover appropriately requires a fundamentally different approach to error-handling than is suggested by the high-level overview provided to the committee. That this problem was "fixed" by increasing a buffer size exposes a security problem (in addition to an availability issue). Merely increasing a buffer size does not guarantee the system will not fail with some unlikely complex combination of existing and proposed flight plans. If there is no proof that the capacity of the buffer cannot be exceeded by a possible set of inputs, then any fixed buffer size could lead to a system failure.

- *Inadequate recovery actions.* The immediate corrective actions taken— increase the buffer size and change operational procedures—are not sufficient to address the problems exposed by this failure. The system design and architecture need to be examined to make the changes necessary to achieve the required availability. That faults occur in such systems is well known, as are the techniques to cope with such faults. A root cause analysis is needed when errors such as these occur in high-reliability systems.

- *Lack of coherent approach to common-mode failures.* A footnote in the document the committee was provided states, "This capability was added to ERAM in the most recent software build (EAC1400) as a result of efforts to address Common Mode failures. This is the change that added the 128 KB buffer and the logic for its use. To date, this fix has prevented four failures."[3] This statement is of concern because common-mode failures are well known and generally the result of a design fault, the most difficult type of fault to tolerate. Making a change that is described as a "fix" suggests that the basic design of ERAM does not have a comprehensive architecture-based approach to common-mode failures. The fact that "this fix has prevented four failures" suggests that common-mode failures are frequent, which is troubling.

---

[1] Dan Whitcomb, FAA Says Air Traffic Computer Was Overwhelmed by U-2 Spy Plane, *Reuters*, May 5, 2014, http://www.reuters.com/article/2014/05/06/us-usa-airport-losangeles-idUSBREA4501C20140506; Laura Stampler, FAA Confirms Spy Plane Caused LAX Chaos, *Reuters*, May 6, 2014, http://time.com/89130/faa-spy-plane-los-angeles/.

[2] FAA, "ZLA Air Traffic Control (ATC) - Summary of Events Surrounding Declaration of ATC Zero at ZLA," 2014; received following committee inquiry.

[3] FAA, "ZLA Air Traffic Control (ATC) - Summary of Events," 2014; received following committee inquiry. See also A. Scott and J. Menn, Exclusive: Air traffic system failure Caused by computer memory shortage, *Reuters.com*, May 12, 2014, http://www.reuters.com/article/2014/05/12/us-airtraffic-bug-exclusive-idUSBREA4B02320140512.

software that likely resulted in many changes to the system (as is appropriate). If there were a system architecture with appropriate data, process, and other perspectives available, then much of the updated functionality could be simulated, modeled, evaluated, and reasoned about.

Rather than being a system that is developed within the conceptual framework of architectures that have been shown to meet requirements, NextGen is instead a collection of projects each aimed at upgrading or replacing existing componentry and capabilities. The upgrades are needed, so NextGen is delivering value. But they are upgrades and enhancements of the existing system, based on the longstanding architectures and designs of the NAS. As such, their ability to meet NextGen's stated objectives and requirements is unknown, and indeed, without an appropriately scaled and specified system architecture, probably unknowable.

**Finding: The FAA's approach to enterprise architecture is not an adequate technical foundation for steering NextGen's technical governance and managing the inevitable changes in technology and operations.**

**Finding: Absent an appropriately scaled and specified system architecture, the ability of any given change, upgrade, or enhancement to meet stated objectives or requirements is unknown and unknowable.**

The committee did learn about the existence of architectural steering groups, but it was not clear how much authority those groups have. Unfortunately, having de facto established the existing architecture as the architecture for NextGen, many opportunities to use the architecture in forward-looking ways have been ruled out. Thus, through its architectural choices, the FAA has put itself in a position where some important advances are going to be extremely challenging to accomplish, such as the ability to create persuasive and credible forecasts of change costs, technical risks, capability upgrades, and performance improvements. The committee's recommendations in this chapter take this into account and offer suggestions as to how move forward most productively in developing better architectural approaches.

## ELEMENTS OF ARCHITECTURAL LEADERSHIP

Any large-scale, software-intensive systems endeavor requires a system architecture that specifies how all of its parts fit together and interact, and which can be used in a dynamic way to help inform and drive planning for change and related decision making. A system architecture provides the capacity to develop and validate analyses that can help detect issues such as single points of failure and emergent properties early in the process. Architectural leadership is essential to the success of any large system of systems, as architecture embodies some of the most important design decisions and includes structural and design commitments that will constrain and guide subsequent expectations and capabilities. Astute architectural leadership encompasses the following elements:

- *Recognition that, although there is a single system architecture, no single architecture perspective is sufficient.* An enterprise perspective (embodied in the NAS enterprise architecture and that sought by OMB) serves different purposes from a software architecture, which is different still from a security architecture, for example.
- *Architectural leadership at the system-of-systems level* to help maintain appropriate alignment among the various architectural perspectives and to ensure that as requirements change and development proceeds that the architecture is kept consistent.
- *Thoughtful and consistent attention to ensuring that the system architecture is flexible and evolvable.*[19] While modernization and incremental improvements proceed, care should be taken to ensure that the architecture does not become too rigid such that innovative changes cannot be put in place later on. A suitable architecture helps to position its users for future flexibility—it can provide an infrastructure that can be exploited for possible (unanticipated) future applications and enables thinking about the future in a structured and disciplined way.
- *Assurance that verification and validation considerations are incorporated early in architectural perspectives.* Verification and validation efforts relate to a wide range of attributes including system functional behavior, security, availability and resilience, performance, response to anomalous human behavior, and so on. Such an approach ensures that the highest value and highest risk elements of system assurance are also addressed earlier in the life cycle.
- *Development and maintenance of effective architectural documentation.* Exhortations for "better architecture" often result only in more volume and more detail, but no more (and sometimes even less) insight and effec-

---

[19] Some efforts go so far as to incorporate an evolution viewpoint to guide the reasoning required for dealing with change. In this approach, points of change, their sources, dependencies among changes and impacts are explicitly managed as first-class entities. See for example, M. Razavian and P. Lago, "A Viewpoint for Dealing with Change in Migration to Services," in *Proceedings of the Joint 10th Working IEEE/IFIP Conference on Software Architecture and 6th European Conference on Software Architecture (WICSA/ECSA)*, IEEE Computer Society, http://ieeexplore.ieee.org, 2012.

tive guidance. This is not what the committee advocates. NextGen architectural leadership should focus instead on identifying system features and aspects that have the highest value (taking into account cost) or represent the greatest risk (see Chapter 3), and align technical projects with a coherent understanding of structural, operational, and performance intentions. An architecture that is documented in an effective useful manner is easier to understand, analyze, maintain, update, and use.[20]

- *A practice of effective architecture evaluation.* Both effective documentation and architecture are encouraged through periodic reviews (architecture evaluation).[21]

- *A common understanding of key performance parameters, along with models to assess how each would be affected by various alternative choices within NextGen.*[22] In NextGen, such key performance parameters might include the ability to incorporate large growth in UAS, or versions of stated goals such as shorter routes, improved navigation around weather, reduced time and fuel costs, reduced delays, increased airport capacity and so on. These may need to be traded against each other, but doing so is best done transparently.[23]

- *Attention to cost and sustainability.* A key aspect of architecting in the large, beyond devising technical solutions and approaches, is feasible, cost-effective, sustainable solutions. In any large-scale system there will be numerous trade-offs, just as there are numerous risks (discussed in

---

[20] For a given system, such as NextGen, there may be several descriptions of the architecture used for different purposes. Ideally, these should be kept consistent, but each may have different details and emphases. Some will be used for communication among projects and with stakeholders, others for specification of how things must be done in component systems, for planning, budgeting, and so on. To serve multiple purposes an architecture description should be explicitly linked from its stakeholders (who cares?) to their concerns (what do they care about?) to the viewpoints framing those concerns (how are these aspects of the architecture modeled?) to the views and models comprising the descriptions (how are the concerns of the stakeholders addressed?).

[21] P. Clements, R. Kazman, and M. Klein, *Evaluating Software Architectures: Methods and Case Studies*, SEI Series, Addison-Wesley, 2002; H. Obbink et al. *Report on Software Architecture Review and Assessment (SARA)*, Tech. Rep. Version 1.0, The SARA Working Group, February 2002.

[22] The existence of such models is noted as a key success pattern in the 2008 NRC report *Pre-Milestone A and Early-Phase Systems Engineering*.

[23] Many of these potential key performance parameters are still up for debate and potential trades even though the NextGen effort has been under way for quite some time. Resolving which of the (many, shifting) implicit and explicit goals of NextGen should be key performance parameters is beyond the scope of this committee's tasking. Instead, the committee has focused on the importance of a suitable architectural approach—regardless of which key performance parameters are chosen—to make progress. A stronger architectural foundation will also make it possible to explore the relationship between the key parameters and the system design.

the next chapter). Architecture leadership should aim to devise solutions that are feasible, fit within budget, and minimize disruption to existing operations.

- *An architectural community with growing diversity of thought, perspective, and knowledge.* In the committee's view, there is too much reliance at the FAA on tacit knowledge in the heads of a very small number of heroic architects. Developing and retaining a "deeper bench" of talent to grow FAA architectural capability is essential.

## RECOMMENDATIONS TO IMPROVE ARCHITECTURE AND ARCHITECTURAL LEADERSHIP

The most important thing on which the FAA should focus with respect to architecture is building a community of architecture leaders within and outside the agency. The FAA will need to increase its system architecture capabilities and establish a more capable architecture community. Good architects will tailor the efforts effectively, independent of the processes, methods, and artifacts with which they need to work. Architectural leadership requires creative skills and abstract reasoning coupled with domain experience. The imposition of additional process requirements or more training will not significantly help to transform an average systems engineer into a capable architect. Developing an effective architectural leadership team is more of a selection and hiring challenge than it is a training issue. Major software companies and system integrators have highly evolved career paths, mentoring programs, and peer selection boards in place to identify, develop, and certify qualified architects. The FAA and its contractor community could learn much from commercial practice in building stronger communities of architectural leadership.

Good architects need to be empowered with authority, within a suitable organizational structure, to succeed. The committee's impression is that on many projects (particularly when OMB rules are in play), architecting is treated as a parallel activity to engineering and development with an emphasis on producing the mandated artifacts. Successful architects often must negotiate requirements, influence acquisition, change budgets, and recommend significant changes on-the-fly. Unfortunately, traditional project management structures are often not conducive to "architecture-centric" efforts. Much can be learned from commercial practices (such as in software development), although some of these have the advantage of being single-product oriented efforts. Another important model, for systems of this scale, is the city planner model, which empowers planners via legislation and building codes.

As discussed in the section above on architectural leadership, more intellectual leadership, diversity of thought and approach, and more people challenging the status quo with good ideas are needed. FAA's contractor community itself possesses some of the necessary architectural skills and expertise and could be harnessed to help provide input to the overall NAS architecture design and evolution. The FAA could leverage the relationships it already has with contractors working on particular systems and components and solicit higher-level input and advice from them while not abdicating its own overall responsibility for the architecture.

One challenge is that while such a community would be helpful in long-range, pre-competitive environments (pre-RFP), there is little incentive for contractors competing for work to share their best ideas in multi-stakeholder forums. Addressing this structural issue will be a challenge. Some consideration should be given to the nature of how the architects are organized. The FAA may need to structure an alignment, for its contractors, of decision authority and responsibility that incentivizes them both to participate in this collective process and to share responsibility for outcomes. One successful model—rarely found in government projects, but found in building architecture—separates the organizations responsible for architecting from organizations responsible for implementation or operation and separates architect from client. The architect works for the client and oversees and certifies implementation. The architect's role is especially critical in managing "systemic properties," such as security, safety, availability, end-to-end performance, information management, and interoperability, across the portfolio of NAS elements in a coherent manner.

The architecture leadership will need to prioritize—focusing on those properties considered systemic and on the evolvability of the system as a whole, while delegating implementation choices to specific programs. Some government agencies create advisory panels or similar constructs to review and comment on plans and efforts. In the FAA's case, it would be important to ensure that there are technically competent people, however the leadership community is created, who are familiar with system architecture and help stimulate creative thinking. One downside of advisory panels as typically structured is that they do not have an explicit stake in the outcome of the development or responsibility to stay with an effort if it goes astray. In whatever form it takes, an architecture leadership community is a locus within which to accomplish the following:

- Provide leadership regarding requirements negotiation, acquisition, budgeting, verification and validation, testing and certification, acceptance, integration, and key changes and their anticipated effects on the system as a whole.
- Define coherent overarching technical objectives to provide direction to incremental program steps.

- Manage and communicate horizontal dependencies better.
- Design and develop an architecture for change, incorporating both flexibility and evolvability, so as to be ready for unanticipated demands or changes in requirements. These changes may range from new hazards that will need to be modeled to new requirements imposed by legislation. Architectural models will need to manage a variety of potential constraints on the architecture.
- Determine appropriate approaches to information hiding and abstraction to support basic system infrastructure services. For example, the NextGen architecture does not address availability or cybersecurity in a comprehensive way, which in part derives from this lack of infrastructure abstraction.[24] By abstracting infrastructure aggressively, the system avoids reliance on particular hardware choices, but can instead allow the hardware (and some systems layers above, perhaps) to stay current with mainstream computational infrastructure. If managed well, this confers the benefit of lower infrastructural operations and maintenance costs and the added advantage of a steady increase in capacity to meet rises in demand.
- Ensure that suitable methods are in use for aggregating systemic properties from the levels at which they are understood to higher levels of abstraction where they can be managed.[25]
- Ensure that mechanisms are in place to discover and share architectural techniques. There are multiple technical and engineering fields that are relevant and which have value to large, complex, software-intensive efforts such as NextGen. A key insight that architects can provide is that complex systems entail multiple concerns, and therefore require a multidisciplinary approach.
- Communicate changing circumstances and reset expectations among stakeholders as needed (as described in Chapter 1)—perhaps the most important activity for which the community will be well positioned. A critical role of an effective architecture community is two-fold: (1) playing offense by assessing new features, new value propositions, and deployment plans and persuading stakeholders with proposed changes that improve efficiency or effectiveness of the system and (2) playing defense by quantifying and prioritizing critical risks, trading off mitiga-

---

[24] The need to pay attention to availability was well illustrated by the recent ERAM failure described in Box 2.1. Just as security should begin with a threat model, design for availability should start with a comprehensive hazard analysis and proceed with suitable models of mitigation based on architectural specifics.

[25] System-level issues such as safety, availability, and the like are typically assessed at the level of individual systems. It will be important to address these techniques at the system architecture level. Although there is progress in this area, generally, that sort of abstraction is also still very much an ongoing research topic.

tion approaches, and designing solutions that fit within programmatic constraints.
- Tap into the best ideas available worldwide, in public and private sector organizations, for air traffic control and airspace management.

To be clear, the committee does not urge the premature creation of more detailed specifications and artifacts absent deeper insights and stronger analyses of risks and trade-offs. In many ways, such efforts would be counterproductive, translating into more overhead (process and documentation) and less attention, resources, and expertise focused on better design, decisions, tests, and earlier integration. One failure pattern in the systems and software industry that the FAA should strive to avoid is building an extremely precise version of plans, scope, and architecture, with only an imprecise understanding of likely trade-offs, user needs, or the team's capability. Additional premature precision often ultimately translates into future rework and waste.

There are some areas where commitments need to be deferred. Uncertainties associated with these deferred decisions can be encapsulated using suitably designed abstractions. Specific commitments should be deferred until the choice is both necessary to make and well informed (through precedent, modeling, simulation, prototyping, or other means) and both the likelihood and extent of adverse consequence of a wrong commitment are reduced. Hence, the committee's emphasis on abstraction—exposing appropriate information and functionality at appropriate levels—and perspective.[26] Documentation practices, and architecting in general, should be agile: the simplest thing that works with an emphasis on minimal documentation targeted to specific needs of specific stakeholders.

Balance with regard to both documentation and technical commitments is important. Finding an appropriate balance between the level of specific technical commitment in a system-architectural model (with all the benefits of fixing on particular choices in this regard) and the ability to respond to the continuing rapid evolution of technology and infrastructure is key. This ability to respond is determined both by the quality of the abstractions built in to the architectural models (at any given moment) and the nimbleness of the process for updating and evolving the architecture. An unfortunate pattern that can result is that "architecture" will come to refer to a set of enduring standards that are generally divorced from the current state of technology and that, consequently, cannot yield the intended benefits of a true system architecture.

---

[26] Additional precision and detail can and should be added incrementally at appropriate levels as sharper perceptions and more solid understandings evolve.

Governance and appropriate authorities are vital for developing an effective architecture. The previous section noted the lack of explicit connection between "leaf nodes" in the enterprise architecture and the program-level architectures. The programs will need to be compliant with specifications in the higher-level architecture and show clearly how they satisfy it—but facilitating such compliance does not require detailed specifications of all the programs in the architecture itself. Because programs are developed by other parts of the FAA that are not under control of the NextGen office, there needs to be a decision authority—informed and guided by an able architecture leadership community—to enforce governance.

The architectural leadership should be responsible for balancing tensions among a number of competing goals, such as innovation and stability or safety, value delivered and costs incurred, security and openness, uncertainty and predictability, process maturity and agility, and so on—avoiding an excessively bureaucratic process- and document-bound approach while providing sufficient leadership and direction. Governance will be needed to facilitate an effective process by which issues can be raised, debated, decided, recorded, and implemented. There are obvious potential complications and conflicts of interest in involving architects from contractors, from other agencies, and from among and between different FAA projects. Without appropriate architectural governance and enforcement, involving the industry's stakeholders, the community will fail to exert influence on NAS development.

Commercial practice has long recognized the need for nurturing and identifying strong architectural skills. Global systems integrators and large government contractors have disciplined programs for technical career paths that attract professionals with exceptional skills for architecting, research, and innovation. For example, IBM has evolved corporate standards for technical roles and technical career paths, including systems and software architects. These prestigious positions are achieved through years of apprenticeship, a track record of accomplishment, and selection by a certification board composed of technical peers. Job titles such as "distinguished engineer" and "fellow" reflect highly influential roles that have executive standing within companies like IBM and Microsoft.

An architectural community represents a set of eclectic skills coupled with deep domain experience. Relatively few engineering-trained professionals can excel in architectural decision making.[27] For such a scarce resource, the FAA will be challenged to attract and retain such talent. The

---

[27] For instance, at IBM where there is a very large pool of technical employees—greater than 100,000—the percentage of distinguished engineers and fellows is less than 1 percent of the technical population.

financial incentives and dynamic opportunities of commercial markets are significantly more attractive. Therefore, the FAA will need to look externally for these skills in resource pools such as academia, systems integrators, and professional societies.

The committee believes that the NextGen challenge represents a unique and attractive technical opportunity for qualified architects. NextGen is a world-class challenge with broad impact on the livelihoods of many people and a cornerstone of our way of life. It is the sort of system that easily ends up making news on the front page of every national newspaper if it works well, or if it does not. Marketing this opportunity and channeling the best of the available talent pool will require some technical leadership and compensation models that are foreign to the FAA and government contracts. The technical steering and technical governance model of the NAS requires some innovative thinking.

**Recommendation: The Federal Aviation Administration (FAA) should initiate, grow, and engage a capable architecture community—leaders and peers within and outside FAA—who will expand the breadth and depth of expertise that is steering architectural changes.**

**Recommendation: The Federal Aviation Administration should conduct a small number of experiments among its system integration partners to prototype candidate solutions for establishing and managing a vibrant architectural community.**

**Recommendation: The Federal Aviation Administration should use an architecture leadership community and an effective governance approach to assure a proper balance between documents and artifacts and to provide high-level guidance and a capability that (1) enables effective management and communication of dependencies, (2) provides flexibility and evolvability to ensure accommodation of future needs, and (3) communicates changing circumstances in order to align expectations.**

# 3

# Cope with Change

The National Airspace System (NAS) is a critical infrastructure for the United States. In concert with revising the architectural approach for the Next Generation Air Transportation System (NextGen), planning to cope with change is needed. Change can be thought of as the ongoing management of trade-offs, which are not clearly identified in the existing tacit architecture (discussed in Chapter 2). Indeed, any system architecture developed will need to reflect planning for resilience in order to encapsulate anticipated variability. This chapter discusses cybersecurity, unmanned aircraft systems (UAS), and safety to illustrate why planning for resilience in the NextGen is so important. The chapter then lays out a broader framework for thinking through resilience and risk management for software-intensive systems such as NextGen.

## CYBERSECURITY

As the committee noted in its interim report,[1] the designers and developers of any software- and communications-intensive system deployed today must grapple with questions of cybersecurity.[2] Understanding

---

[1] National Research Council (NRC), *Interim Report of a Review of the Next Generation Air Transportation System Enterprise Architecture, Software, Safety, and Human Factors*, The National Academies Press, Washington, D.C., 2014.

[2] Here the committee refers to what some call cybersecurity (system, data, and communications security), which is distinct from the physical security required for airport and aircraft operation, provided in part by the Transportation Security Administration (TSA).

cybersecurity risks and threats and developing appropriate threat models and mitigations are challenges endemic across government and industry. NextGen is no exception; indeed, the safety-of-life implications and the vital economic importance of air travel make the security of NextGen and the NAS critically important. As various programs and components of the NAS are modernized, upgraded, and transformed, the security implications of the changes will need to be taken into account. The criticality of cybersecurity for NextGen increases as more services rely on digital technologies, networked communications, and commercial-off-the-shelf software.

Although acknowledging an increase in risk as they move to new, more connected technologies, the Federal Aviation Administration (FAA) staff noted in briefings to the committee that they rely heavily on federal guidelines for cybersecurity support. For example, the FAA relies on the National Institute of Standards and Technology risk management framework,[3] and the Department of Transportation Inspector General and Government Accountability Office (GAO) periodically audit the compliance with federal and FAA security orders, directives, and guidance.

FAA staff stated that the enterprise-level programs address specific information threats; however, they also state that there are no current NAS-level threat models. Furthermore, from what the committee has learned, information security is not currently a consideration during safety analysis. FAA staff did note that the current safety management manual was in revision, and there are plans to address the exclusion of security. The FAA also noted that threats are addressed at the program level, and all major programs must comply with federal guidelines on information security, and information security is a component of the acquisition management life cycle. NAS-level threats are expected to be addressed through these enterprise-level programs. For example, the committee was told that information security is an integral part of the acquisition management life cycle. The committee was also briefed on a proposed NextGen cybersecurity test facility, which would provide some initial movement toward eventual capability.[4]

The committee remains concerned that cybersecurity, although acknowledged as an issue and with some efforts under way to address

---

Cybersecurity efforts may themselves require physical security components, such as physical safeguards to servers, data centers, and workers, to mitigate various kinds of threats.

[3] National Institute of Standards and Technology, *Framework for Improving Critical Infrastructure Cybersecurity. Version 1.0*, February 12, 2014, http://www.nist.gov/cyberframework/upload/cybersecurity-framework-021214.pdf.

[4] Federal Aviation Administration (FAA), "ANG-B3 Proposed NextGEN Cyber Security Test Facility: Analysis and Research of Common Cyber Security Requirements," presented to the committee on February 19, 2014.

it, has not been fully integrated into the agency's thinking, planning, and efforts with respect to NextGen and the NAS generally (although it recognizes that some of these efforts may be subject to classification, and therefore, the committee may not have a complete view). Because of the scale of the NAS, hazard analysis for security must be undertaken for individual subsystems and components within the system rather than just at a notion of a "perimeter." This is an important consideration for any larger-scale system and particularly systems that are interconnected with other systems. That is, internal service interfaces must be designed to be resilient against the possibility that other parts of the system may be controlled by adversaries. In addition, as new technologies and procedures are rolled out, there will inevitably be new vulnerabilities (this is true for any information technology (IT)-based system and is not specific to the FAA). Moreover, changes in the way existing, long-stable technologies are used may introduce new security issues. There may also be vulnerabilities associated with avionics governed by international standards. So, threat analyses in both dimensions—on existing systems and associated standards with any expected changes, and on new components—are needed. Threat analysis should encompass both the nature of threats in the operating environment and the security-focused hazard analysis that connects the understanding of possible threats with architectural decisions. For these reason, cybersecurity will need to be managed architecturally. Individual threat analyses of programs need to be "rolled up" to an architectural threat model, and that threat model also needs to be potentially checked on each program.

In the committee's view, as systems are increasingly digital and dependent on communications and networks, and as the threat landscape for the nation as a whole continues to evolve, cybersecurity will need to be an important and integral part of safety activities and is an ongoing operational matter (not only a question of design and architecture). The committee saw little evidence of adequate measures to defend systems against various kinds of attack. Data fusion of wide-area multilateration (WAM)[5] with Automatic Dependent Surveillance-Broadcast (ADS-B) and radar tracks, often cited as an important systemic hedge against certain sorts of attacks (e.g., spoofing), is not a sufficient safeguard because it only protects against a certain class of attacks.

---

[5] Wide-area multilateration is a surveillance capability that "works by employing multiple small remote sensors throughout an area to compensate for terrain obstructions ... the data from multilateration sensors is fused to determine aircraft position and identification" (FAA, "Wide Area Multilateration (WAM) Project," last modified August 19, 2014, http://www.faa.gov/nextgen/programs/adsb/wsa/wam/).

Consistent with the committee's observations, a March 2015 GAO[6] report noted:

> The weaknesses in FAA's security controls and implementation of its security program existed, in part, because FAA had not fully established an integrated, organization-wide approach to managing information security risk that is aligned with its mission. [...] FAA has established a Cyber Security Steering Committee to provide an agency-wide risk management function. However, it has not fully established the governance structure and practices to ensure that its information security decisions are aligned with its mission. For example, it has not (1) clearly established roles and responsibilities for information security for the NAS or (2) updated its information security strategic plan to reflect significant changes in the NAS environment, such as increased reliance on computer networks.
>
> Until FAA effectively implements security controls, establishes stronger agency-wide information security risk management processes, fully implements its NAS information security program, and ensures that remedial actions are addressed in a timely manner, the weaknesses GAO identified are likely to continue, placing the safe and uninterrupted operation of the nation's air traffic control system at increased and unnecessary risk.

The system architecture for the NAS and its future goals need to embrace comprehensive, system-wide measures to ensure cybersecurity. Some cybersecurity requirements are new, based on the fact that some upgrades are using new (e.g., digital) technologies, and the requirements to meet some risks (e.g., Internet-based hacking) are themselves new. So there are new risks, and new requirements that these risks be met and mitigated. Reasoning about such risks will need to be based on clearly stated goals and requirements. Reasoning about risk assessment will become increasingly thorough and definitive as development proceeds through architecture, design, and eventual implementation, although there will always be significant uncertainty. The absence of such architectures precludes the possibility of such reasoning and leaves doubt about the exact security capabilities that NextGen will be able to achieve. Cybersecurity requires a system-wide approach that is managed architecturally and cannot be addressed piecemeal by each contractor (or program) separately. Nor can security be added to the system later. Safety properties themselves are dependent on a resilient, trustworthy, secure system, so careful integration of cybersecurity models and processes into safety analysis will

---

[6] Government Accountability Office, *Information Security: FAA Needs to Address Weaknesses in Air Traffic Control Systems*, GAO-15-221, publicly released March 2, 2015, http://www.gao.gov/products/GAO-15-221.

become increasingly important. Finally, cybersecurity itself is an ongoing challenge in many domains and the subject of ongoing research; it will be important to track and integrate relevant results as the field continues to evolve.

Finding: Cybersecurity is critical to the NextGen and the NAS. Cybersecurity challenges extend from major software platforms into the specification and design of embedded (avionics) equipment that connects directly to the NAS. The cybersecurity challenge for the NAS is a direct consequence of increasingly digital communications and systems.

Finding: Although there will always be risk, the lack of appropriate architectural approaches to security and safety that allow for reasoning about risks and uncertainty only increase the likelihood that risks of unknown magnitude can remain embedded in the NAS.

Recommendation: The Federal Aviation Administration (FAA) should incorporate cybersecurity as systems characteristic at all levels of the architecture and design. The FAA should begin by developing a threat model followed by an appropriate set of architectural and design concepts that will mitigate the associated risks, support resilience in the face of attack or compromise, and allow for dynamic evolution to meet a changing threat environment. The FAA should inculcate a cybersecurity mindset complementary to its well-established safety mindset throughout the organization, its contractors, and leadership.

## UNMANNED AIRCRAFT SYSTEMS

The FAA defines a UAS as "an unmanned aircraft and its associated elements related to safe operations, which may include control stations (ground-, ship-, or air-based), control links, support equipment, payloads, flight termination systems, and launch/recovery equipment."[7] The FAA Reauthorization Act of 2012 calls for the safe integration of UAS in the NAS by 2015. Several interim steps have been taken, including the establishment of six UAS test sites and the first roadmap for the integration of

---

[7] FAA, *Integration of Civil Unmanned Aircraft Systems (UAS) in the National Airspace System (NAS) Roadmap*, November 7, 2013.

UAS that reflects near-, mid-, and long-term integration activities.[8] The FAA also recently proposed rules for small UAS.[9]

UAS are already in use as hobbyist craft, and the FAA estimates that thousands of small UAS could be active over the next 5 years.[10] Many of these will be small operations—flying below 500 feet, within line of sight, or away from controlled airspace—and not require air traffic services. Small UAS have the potential for significant economic impact; examples include surveying and treating crops fields, local news reporting, or supporting local law enforcement operations. When additional guidance is in place, higher-altitude operations that fly above 500 feet, are beyond line of sight, or that need civil airspace infrastructure will presumably need to be equipped with applicable technologies to interact with current and future air traffic services.

Several NextGen technologies are essential to the safe integration of UAS: the NAS voice system, which will allow UAS pilots to communicate with air traffic control (ATC) over ground-to-ground communication networks; Data Communications (Data Comm), which will support the sending of digital messages to the flight crew; and System Wide Information Management, which will support more timely and improved information access to all users of the NAS. However, NextGen planning and architecture did not explicitly anticipate the introduction of UAS and, indeed, the de facto system architecture, having substantially predated the advent of UAS, does not seem to lend itself to incorporating these new types of aircraft that will place new demands on the system.[11] The expected integration of UAS into the NAS will present new safety issues stemming from increased reliance on data links, limited operator sensory and environmental cues, and so on. And insufficiently developed

---

[8] A 2014 Department of Transportation (DOT) Inspector General report on FAA's progress notes that the FAA faces large delays in the integration and that "delays are due to unresolved technological, regulatory, and privacy issues, which will prevent FAA from meeting Congress' September 30, 2015, deadline for achieving safe UAS integration." (DOT, *FAA Faces Significant Barriers to Safely Integrate Unmanned Aircraft Systems into the National Airspace System*, Office of Inspector General Audit Report AV-2014-061, June 26, 2014, https://www.oig.dot.gov/library-item/31975.

[9] FAA, "Overview of Small UAS Notice of Proposed Rulemaking," released February 15, 2015, http://www.faa.gov/uas/nprm/; and FAA, *FAA Aerospace Forecast Fiscal Years 2013-2033*, 2013, https://www.faa.gov/about/office_org/headquarters_offices/apl/aviation_forecasts/aerospace_forecasts/2013-2033/, p. 66.

[10] See FAA, *FAA Aerospace Forecast: Fiscal Years 2014-2034*, 2014, https://www.faa.gov/about/office_org/headquarters_offices/apl/aviation_forecasts/aerospace_forecasts/2014-2034/media/2014_FAA_Aerospace_Forecast.pdf, p. 65.

[11] The FAA's deputy administrator was quoted saying that UAS "weren't really part of the equation when you go back to the origin of NextGen" in J. Lowy, Drones left out of air traffic plans, *AP News*, September 23, 2014. http://bigstory.ap.org/article/d2f90d7230af40b493a849df06e7512e/ap-exclusive-drones-left-out-air-traffic-plans.

system architecture is one of several obstacles to fully integrating UAS into the NAS.

The integration of UAS is an example of a rapidly emerging requirement that could provoke disruptive changes to both technology and to roles and responsibilities. Allowing detect-and-avoid capability (versus see-and-avoid) will require changes to the roles of pilot and controller. Emergency procedures will need to be developed and tested (e.g., loss of data link).[12] There are privacy issues that arise, as well as questions about airworthiness and associated certifications. And, related to the discussion of cybersecurity above, the introduction of UAS into the NAS will be another security risk that will need to addressed in the security architecture and mitigated. Further, low-altitude UAS operations will require new thinking because most are passing through the usual airspace. UAS missions and operations may be considerably different in their location and flight plan (e.g., they may survey an area, rather than transit through a space). Finally, some degree of autonomy in UAS operations may become increasingly desirable, which would generate a variety of new challenges for NAS and NextGen planning.[13]

The committee urges that the FAA use UAS as a use case for developing a better approach to system architecture (and associated technical and procedural designs). As one example, satellite-based surveillance (ADS-B Out and ADS-B In), if fully deployed, allows a different class of solutions to UAS. A living system architecture that appropriately integrates technology and procedural planning could be used to make claims about how the overall system will react (and possibly need to be changed) in response to the new usage model presented by UAS. Are the data requirements alone—content and update rate—for ADS-B Out and ADS-B In sufficient to provide safe operations absent a pilot in the cockpit? And has this been modeled and verified in the system architecture?

> **Finding: The challenge of integrating UAS into the NAS illustrates the challenges of accommodating changing requirements within the current approach to managing architectural and system evolution.**
>
> **Finding: One measure of the quality of the NAS architecture is (and will be) its flexibility in addressing UAS operations as they unfold, recognizing that UAS requirements and capabilities are likely to change a great deal as these technologies mature.**

---

[12] See the 2014 NRC report *Autonomy Research for Civil Aviation: Toward a New Era of Flight* (The National Academies Press, Washington, D.C.).
[13] NRC, *Autonomy Research for Civil Aviation*, 2014.

Recommendation: The Federal Aviation Administration (FAA) and its architecture leadership community should look for and apply lessons from the challenge of integrating unmanned aircraft systems (UAS) into the National Airspace System (NAS) as it develops an effective system architecture. The FAA and its architecture leadership community should incorporate measures in the NAS system architecture to address UAS integration.

## SAFETY IN NEXTGEN AND EMERGENT SYSTEM PROPERTIES

The FAA and the United States rightly pride themselves on a devotion to safety and an excellent safety record to match. At the same time, a conservative safety culture can affect how quickly process and technological change can happen—a challenge in an arena where technologies change rapidly. Such a culture may inhibit the adoption of new technologies or increased automation that could potentially result in net improvements in both safety and efficiency. A strong safety culture can make up for some limitations in an architecture. For example, while it is a good thing for controllers and pilots to be highly sensitive to close-calls, it would be better if the architecture and design precluded those near-misses from happening. Moreover, if the FAA is going to be held accountable for an extremely conservative safety culture—which has historically been the case—then it should be recognized that such conservatism will understandably bias the agency away from innovation. Thus, there are risks associated with a safety culture as well, not least of which are opportunity costs due to not deploying improved (and potentially even safer) technology and procedures in the long run. In addition, excessive care regarding safety can result in the accumulation of technical debt—the deferral of significant refactoring and infrastructure refresh.

The original Joint Planning and Development Office (JPDO) vision of improved safety as a result of NextGen systems and technology has not been realized. The "safety management system" used by the FAA is generally very good for airborne systems but less so for ground systems. One issue with ground systems can be seen in a recent ERAM failure (discussed in Chapter 2) and in the National Transportation Safety Board's annual appeal for better technology to prevent runway incursions.

Safety engineering is about reducing residual risk as low as possible and certainly below a threshold of acceptability. Safety engineers do not cease analysis just because a system's operational record is satisfactory. Any accident, especially loss of a commercial transport, is regarded as an extremely serious event to be avoided. With that view in mind, the modernization efforts under way in NextGen raise two key countervailing safety issues:

1. *The opportunity to exploit the overall system information infrastructure to further reduce residual risk.* This opportunity has not been well exploited. An enterprise architecture, for example, could have provided clear data architectural views to allow discovery of single points of failure in the system[14] and to expose data limits that would cause the system to perform in ways not designed.[15]
2. *New practices and procedures made available by NextGen will transform a system with an excellent record into a new system with no operational record (even if the change is incremental).* This is, in part, because even for incremental changes, there are at least four implementation cycles, all of which pose some risk: keeping the current state functional; updating and upgrading today's NAS with existing technology; updating the NAS system with future technology; and the implementation of these changes along the way. All change has some risk; the fact that process and procedure must be changed multiple times, especially when there is not a system approach to the architecture (discussed in Chapter 2), creates difficulties. In such circumstances, a comprehensive analysis of the residual risk that results from the change, coupled with precise system operational monitoring until confidence in risk levels is established, will be important.

The early JPDO vision focused on the first item. At present, there are systems such as minimum safe altitude warning (MSAW) that are designed to provide supplementary information to ATC about hazardous states. ADS-B and wide area augmentation system (WAAS), for example, provide a major improvement in the information available to ATC over what has been available with radars. That NextGen does not have a system-wide monitoring system above and beyond things like MSAW, traffic collision avoidance system (TCAS), and enhanced ground proximity warning system (EGPWS) is surprising. New sensors and communications and computing capabilities suggest that additional monitoring—of hazardous states and states that existing sensors are expected to detect—will be important.

The second item poses more challenges to safety analysis. With new practices and procedures, even if the technology is primarily aimed at upgrading systems in place, there will be emergent properties and behaviors, some of which may create new safety risks. Is it understood and

---

[14] A recent Chicago Center fire took down the whole center by cutting certain communications. The fact that this occurred is made worse by a previous example of single fiber optic cable cut that did the same thing. See James Adams, *The Next World War: Computers Are the Weapons and the Front Line Is Everywhere*, Simon and Shuster, New York, N.Y., 1998, p. 173.

[15] See Box 2.2.

well articulated to stakeholders how changes in the NAS could affect the hazard rate? The committee believes this understanding should be reflected in the system architecture and be readily assessable as proposed changes are considered. Stakeholders should find their concerns reflected explicitly, and there should be models that evaluate safety requirements in terms of the highest-level structural choices in the system. Moreover, stakeholders should also be able to see evidence of evaluation of alternatives. There will also, undoubtedly, be opportunities to take advantage of new approaches to safety engineering that have emerged in recent years—primarily driven by the broad introduction of digital technology.

In architectural terms, safety is, presumably, a key performance parameter. As such, it should be linked to an understanding of how changes in ATC capabilities would affect the accident rate. Those links need to be understood, communicated, and explicitly reflected in the system architecture. A system architecture, as described in Chapter 2, would allow evaluation of things like safety in terms of the highest-level structural choices in the system. And it would enable generation and communication of the evidence of evaluation of alternatives.

## RISK MANAGEMENT

The discussions of cybersecurity and UAS illustrate the need for a dynamic and flexible approach to emerging challenges that will inevitably present themselves over time. Given expected future changes, the architectural capability encouraged in Chapter 2 would offer insights on how such changes could be incorporated and where the highest risks will be. More generally, the NAS will need to be resilient, and the FAA will need to ensure appropriate and effective risk management strategies. Such strategies will need to encompass safety of flight and security, in addition to programmatic, operational, and engineering risk. This section offers a brief overview of the challenges to traditional engineering project management of software-intensive systems. It then focuses briefly on management of software risk in particular, in response to the statement of task, and describes the committee's views on risks to NextGen.

As discussed in Chapter 1, NextGen today implicitly embodies a set of decisions to not dramatically change a wide range of current operations. Those decisions, along with an analysis of their implications, are not explicit in the tacit architecture. But a decision to not change carries heavy implications for the realization of any gains that would require such changes. The 2008 NRC report[16] cited earlier and ISO/IEC/IEEE Standard

---

[16] NRC, *Pre-Milestone A and Early-Phase Systems Engineering*, The National Academies Press, Washington, D.C., 2008.

42010[17] both have a clear perspective on what constitutes good practice in architecting. They presume that the heart of good practice is to explicitly state value attributes (with scales) at the full system, develop multiple alternative architectures (in the sense of systems or systems-of-systems), and have evaluation models that compare those alternatives to the value attributes. Both recommend that multiple alternatives be explored and that the rationale for choice be explicit. The committee was struck by the lack of alternatives articulated for NextGen.

Conventional engineering project management techniques assume little uncertainty in their requirements and exploit mature precedents for construction and deployment. Large-scale software projects managed with such engineering governance models typically uncover changes late in the life cycle that are difficult to manage and spend 40 percent or more of their effort consumed in late scrap and rework.[18] Much of NextGen is focused on new software and the computer platforms it runs on. The iron law of traditional software engineering is this: the later you are in the life cycle, the more expensive things are to fix.[19]

In the committee's experience, project managers who are experienced and trained in traditional project management disciplines such as detailed planning, critical-path analysis, and earned value management may have a particularly rough transition to dealing with these types of projects. They must move from a world of managing certainty and precision to a world of resolving uncertainty based on imprecise probabilistic judgments. Although these ideas are far from new, they are also far from being standard practice in most software enterprises and require management support, leadership, and training to be implemented well. In addition, it can be easy for a program office to go into denial regarding risks, especially without incentives to aggressively seek out and identify uncertainties. Unless such incentives exist, there is likely to be a coupling of engineering risk with overall project risk. Another factor that can make transparent risk assessment and communication difficult could be the technical use of the term "risk" to refer to uncertainties regarding

---

[17] International Organization for Standardization (ISO)/International Electrotechnical Commission (IEC)/Institute of Electrical and Electronics Engineers (IEEE), Standard ISO/IEC/IEEE 42010:2011, "Systems and Software Engineering—Architecture Description," December 2011, http://www.iso.org/iso/catalogue_detail.htm?csnumber=50508.

[18] W. Royce, *Software Project Management: A Unified Framework*, Addison-Wesley, Reading, Mass., 1998.

[19] A study from NASA suggests that costs can increase by more than two orders of magnitude as fault discovery and repair are deferred until later in the life cycle. See J.M. Stecklein, J. Dabney, B. Dick, B. Haskins, R. Lovell, and G. Moroney, "Error Cost Escalation Through the Project Lifecycle," paper presented at 14th Annual International Symposium, June 19, 2004, available http://ntrs.nasa.gov/search.jsp?R=20100036670.

the consequences of potential engineering commitments. There may be counter-incentives in place to present a picture in which "risks" appear to be minimized.

There is a reasonable framing of these sorts of risk-related issues in the new book by Boehm et al., "*The Incremental Commitment Spiral Model: Principles and Practices for Successful Systems and Software*,"[20] which focuses on how engineering uncertainties are identified and resolved, framing the activity as a process of making commitments. The use of the term "risk," while familiar to software and systems engineers, can be misleading to non-practitioners, who might think, "we want to avoid risk," whereas engineers must actively seek identification and engagement with these "risks." It may be useful to think of risk as "engineering uncertainties." An overview of the process is as follows: (1) active identification of uncertainties (part of the ongoing architectural exercise), (2) architecture work to decouple the various categories of uncertainties, (3) identification and consideration of options for handling the various uncertainties (through modeling, simulation, prototyping, etc.), (4) appropriately timed resolution of individual uncertainties (entailing an engineering commitment), and (5) ongoing reconsideration of commitments in response to changes in the operating environment and in the technical infrastructure. All of this is enabled by "good" architectural design, which minimizes the extent of coupling among the various uncertainties and commitments.

However it is phrased, for large-scale, critical initiatives such as NextGen, clear assessments, understanding, and communication of risk are essential. The risk management foundation underlying the modern spiral model and the basic ideas of software engineering economics were first laid out in the 1980s and have been updated over time.[21] Applying probability theory to deal with uncertainty is also well established.[22] As an example of how probability can be helpful in managing risks, consider a project that will move forward in three successive phases, where the duration of each is governed by independent bell-shaped normal distributions. Then the total time to completion is the sum of the three

---

[20] B. Boehm, J.A. Lane, S. Koolmanojwong, and R. Turner, *The Incremental Commitment Spiral Model: Principles and Practices for Successful Systems and Software*, Pearson Education, Upper Saddle River, N.J., 2014.

[21] See B. Boehm, A spiral model of software development and enhancement, *Computer* 21(5):61-72, 1988; B. Boehm, *Software Engineering Economics*, Prentice Hall, 1981; and Boehm et al., *The Incremental Commitment Spiral Model*, 2014. In addition, the 2010 NRC report *Critical Code: Software Producibility for Defense* (The National Academies Press, Washington, D.C.) also discusses the concept of risk in the engineering process.

[22] S. Biffl, A. Aurum, B. Boehm, H. Erdogmus, and P. Grünbacher, eds., *Value-Based Software Engineering*, Springer-Verlag, Berlin Heidelberg, 2006; H. Erdogmus, Valuation of learning options in software development under private and market risk, *Engineering Economist* 47(3):308-353, 2002.

normal random variables, and the total uncertainty—as measured by the standard deviation—is not the sum of the three individual uncertainties (it could be considerably less). Moreover, the probability of completion in any particular time frame (e.g., 3 years) could be specified.

New, iterative development methods have emerged organically from diverse software development communities to improve navigation through uncertainty. Such navigation requires measured improvement with dynamic controls, instrumentation, and intermediate checkpoints that permit stakeholders to assess what they have achieved so far (the as-is situation), what adjustments they should make to the target objectives (the predicted-to-be situation), and how to refactor what they have achieved to adjust those targets in the most economical way (the roadmap forward). The key results could be reduced overhead and a significant reduction (perhaps as high as 50 percent) in scrap and rework.[23]

Uncertainty can be quantified by measuring the reduction in variance in the distribution of resource estimates to complete.[24] A reduction in variance, even when means are unchanged, is an important sort of progress because reduction in uncertainty regarding cost to complete is valuable progress. A reduction in the standard deviation could help reveal how the spread of the distribution around its mean has shrunk. Or, a reduction in the probability of some particularly adverse outcome (which may not be proportional to variance in the distribution of resources) might be a useful quantification. These estimates are random variables and should be represented by their probability distributions, not just the mean values. In a healthy software project, each phase of development produces an increased level of understanding by reducing uncertainty in the evolving plans, specifications, and demonstrable releases. At any point in the life cycle, the precision of the subordinate artifacts, especially the code and test base, should be in balance with the evolving precision in understanding and at compatible levels of detail. Specialists in probability and statistics can play an important, ongoing role in risk management for NextGen. Some such specialists are available to the FAA through the National Center of Excellence in Operations Research.

The risks of NextGen's software development approach are inherently difficult to quantify. However, quantifying risks and value offers means better planning and management. The challenge for complex systems such as NextGen is how to quantify and prioritize risks so that

---

[23] W. Royce, Measuring agility and architectural integrity, *International Journal of Software and Informatics* 5(3):415-433, 2011.

[24] The reduction in variance of a forecasted value is a measure of "validated learning," which is elaborated further in the discussion of entrepreneurial risk management presented in *The Lean Startup: How Today's Entrepreneurs Use Continuous Innovation to Create Radically Successful Businesses* by Eric Reis (Crown Business, New York, N.Y., 2011).

projects can be steered effectively and uncertainties can be systematically resolved earlier in the life cycle. In all engineering projects, and particularly software engineering projects, this usually means understanding as early in the life cycle as possible, the consequences of risky decisions. If the consequences are not understood until late in the process, then the costs of unwinding previous bad decisions may become prohibitive, and the architecture becomes a source of change friction that burdens efficiency of execution. If the consequences can be understood and managed earlier, then the architecture can be effectively refactored and optimized. An effective architecture can be a basis for risk assessment and mitigation and can be used as a tool to support decision making and the recording of decisions.

A good "window" through which one can manage risks and assess the value that NextGen is likely to deliver is inherent in how the FAA's predictions of risk have changed over time. Unfortunately, this window is far too opaque for the committee to draw quantifiable conclusions. The risk management employed by the FAA as described to the committee is heavy on process and procedure, but there is little insight inherent in the artifacts and outcomes of their risk management process. Although requested, the committee did not receive a clear description of the "top five" risks to NextGen and did not receive any quantified representation of the top risks, whether they be schedule, cost, technical, or cultural. In the committee's view, in an environment with an effective risk management process, the top several risks—whatever they were, and there will always be risks—would be well known and internalized by everyone.

With regard to specific risk drivers, the committee observed that some important choices and considerations are driven by what appear to be hardware fixed-points, rather than being driven by a systems architecture. In some ways, the engineering agenda seems to be set by assumptions about hardware procurement (e.g., the hardware selected for ADS and Data Comm). In such a case, incompatibilities, risks, overall system costs, and life-cycle trade-offs might not have been adequately considered and appropriately factored into the decisions that led to the selection of these hardware components and the incurring of their now-sunk costs. There are also risks caused by the protracted development cycles of ATC technologies.[25] These challenges impede prospects for future evolution and impinge significantly on architecture. The current mandates for hardware would have benefited from in-depth architectural appraisal along with an analysis of trade-offs between hardware and software.

---

[25] For instance, ADS-B has been under development since the 1990s and will not be fully in service until the 2020s, and ADS-B was developed with little consideration for cybersecurity concerns.

With regard to the specific question of schedule risk, in the committee's view, the schedule risks in NextGen have multiple sources, including budget, approval, certification, and procedure design. With the exception of resourcing and budgets, architecture can help mitigate these. Risk and project management needs are well served by an effective architecture that can be used for risk assessment and planning. However, the under development a system architecture makes it a challenge to determine how well the overall system will address system requirements (e.g., for security and robustness), causing risks of many kinds, including schedule risks. A conventional cost and schedule risk analysis would need to assess the program variance in reaching particular objectives, but NextGen functional and performance objectives are not really defined, or worse, they are inconsistently understood from stakeholder to stakeholder.

**Finding: The risks to NextGen are not clearly articulated and quantified in order of importance, making it difficult to make sound decisions about how to prioritize effort and allocate resources.**

**Recommendation: The Federal Aviation Administration should use an architecture leadership community and a system architecture, with input from specialists in probability and statistics, as a key tool in managing and mitigating risks and in assessing new value opportunities.**

# 4

# Minimize Cultural and Organizational Barriers

External Next Generation Air Transportation System (NextGen) stakeholders have a variety of interests, demands, and constraints. Agreement, or at least rough consensus, on requirements is important (albeit challenging to achieve). Significant effort is required to ensure that these various interests do not prevent the realization of the public benefits for which the nation has invested. Some NextGen programs and components will undoubtedly have implications for the workforce, especially controllers and pilots. The capacity, skill sets, size, and expectations of the associated workforces must be taken into account when developing and deploying new or changed capabilities.[1]

The Federal Aviation Administration (FAA) has made numerous efforts toward stakeholder engagement. The committee believes that the architecture, if moved in directions as described in early chapters, can be a vital communications tool among all stakeholders. The system architecture should be expressed (documented) in a form that readily facilitates communication, inspection, and debate with stakeholders and advisers. The architecture leadership community that the committee recommends can help ensure that any documentation that is produced is at appropriate levels of abstraction to enable productive discussions among all stakeholders.

---

[1] The 2007 National Research Council (NRC) report *Human-System Integration in the System Development Process: A New Look* (The National Academies Press, Washington, D.C.) explores iterative development processes suitable for systems that have intensive human interaction and with humans having functional roles within the system (e.g., pilots, controllers, and so on).

In addition to the challenges of meeting the needs of a large and diverse stakeholder community, the FAA must contend with internal organizational, cultural, and structural barriers. The rest of this chapter offers the committee's recommendations on a number of related issues: human factors, a look at costs and benefits of NextGen, the challenge of being a system integrator, and the need for sustained support for operations and maintenance.

## HUMAN FACTORS

In any complex system, human factors should be incorporated in design, technical, engineering, and architectural discussions as early as possible.[2] Human factors should not only be addressed after the design is complete (e.g., to check on or tune the design), but much earlier in the process. For the FAA, this is both an organizational challenge—it may not have sufficient human factors personnel to integrate contractors' work with system design—as well as a technical and engineering challenge—to determine how requirements and constraints flow to early-stage technical requirements so that human factors perspectives can contribute to early design work. When human factors are not included at the outset, products and services need to be modified subsequently to meet the human factors requirements, which then delays the release of products and services and significantly increases cost.

NextGen depends on existing technology and future development and on creating processes for both to work together. Consequently, human factors efforts will be retroactive in some cases while simultaneously looking to the future. The National Airspace System (NAS) has many moving parts that are being upgraded and updated. Thus, a challenge of human factors is the introduction of concepts while the system is being maintained, upgraded with existing technology, and then being further updated with newer technology. This complexity reinforces the need for human factors input at all phases.

Although human factors expertise exists within a research group in the NextGen organization[3] and in the safety organization, there seems to

---

[2] The use of the term *human factors* in this report is meant to encompass more modern terms such as "human-system interaction" (HSI) and "user experience design" (UX). Attention to the entirety of the interaction, including protocol, robustness (against human error, human inattention, etc.), visualization, affordances, and so on, is needed. The business of "human factors" goes well beyond response latencies and interfaces "on the screen" such as pixels and fonts.

[3] The Human Factors Research and Engineering Division (ANG-C1) is located within the NextGen Advanced Concepts and Development Office (FAA, February 2015 Organizational Chart, http://www.faa.gov/about/office_org/headquarters_offices/ang/offices/media/orgChartANG.pdf).

be no human factors representation at higher levels of NextGen management to participate in and sign off on designs and to track and ensure contractor inclusion of appropriate human factors considerations in implementation. This lack has apparently existed at NextGen from the beginning. Human factors has played an insufficiently substantive role in the design integration of NextGen systems and procedures. Human factors seems to be viewed as research and as relevant to testing and integration but not as a significant part of system design—and certainly not as a core activity. And given the traditionally late integration of human factors expertise, this is understandable. But NextGen poses a major human factors system design problem—namely, developing confidence through participation in design and simulation, especially for off-nominal scenarios that enable controllers and pilots to understand the capabilities and limits of NextGen capabilities and be able to perform without undue workload, delay, or error.

The human factors research group operates a high-quality laboratory at the Atlantic City Tech Center. That laboratory conducts human-in-the-loop simulations (HITLS) on selected early-stage concepts. In addition, it sponsors some university research and publishes reports that are made available to whomever would like to read them. In addition, NASA Ames Research Center conducts human factors and simulation research (including HITLS) in its Aeronautical Research Division. (A recent example focused on terminal sequencing and spacing.[4]) However, research is not system design, and individuals involved in those projects are too few to participate in any meaningful way in the many stove-piped programs charged with generating design specifications or contracting for and testing of component subsystems of NextGen. The committee's understanding is that ANG-C1 human factors experts are not invited to reviews, and those in the programs often do not know that experts are available. The human factors research group is occasionally asked to help review such designs, but without any formal sign-off responsibility. When human factors experts are not involved in the very early stages of technology and procedure design, a likely result is that many systems (displays, controls, procedures, and subsystems) will not be subject to human factor critiques until contractors take over, if then.

Changes in equipment and procedures beget human errors. The proven means to uncover unintended and unexpected events in human-

---

[4] See, for instance, J. Thipphavong, J. Jung, H. Swenson, L. Martin, M. Lin, and J. Nguyen, "Evaluation of the Terminal Sequencing and Spacing System for Performance-Based Navigation Arrivals," paper presented at 32nd Digital Avionics Systems Conference (DASC), October 2013, available at http://www.aviationsystemsdivision.arc.nasa.gov/publications/atd1/tech-transfer/index.shtml.

system interactions prior to operational deployment is by HITLS. Full-fidelity HITLS can be expensive and time consuming. The FAA has done, or is planning to do, a few of these and cites cost as the main reason for not doing more. However, for purposes of learning, particularly for uncovering unexpected issues of multi-system, multi-person interactions, full fidelity is not necessary. One can gain a great deal from part-task simulations or even what are called "cognitive walk-throughs." The latter are play-acting exercises where an experimenter confederate plays the part of another human (pilot, controller), and the "equipment" is a crude mockup. These exercises would be much less costly than full-fidelity HITLS and could provide useful early-stage input into design and requirements.

One might like to use fast-time analytic models and simulations, but unfortunately there are few human-system analytic models that are very predictive, and they are also very context sensitive. There are very few analytic models that are up to being very helpful for NextGen, other than for modeling basic vision and hearing. One highly relevant model is that the time required for a human to receive an alert of some abnormality, understand the issue, make a decision, and take proper action exhibits a probability distribution with a very long "right-hand tail."[5] There is hard evidence for this. It means that when a human is a serial element in a system, even though the mean and median response times may be short, the wait time required to achieve 95 or 99 percent confidence will be very long.

Human factors has an important role to play in the FAA program management of system engineering and in acquisition. The research group in Atlantic City is used primarily for advanced concept exploration and testing and tuning of systems as they are deployed. The group is not currently used as part of system design, which is done by contractors, nor does it have direct input or sign-off authority in acquisition decisions. However, an FAA human factors group could represent the FAA workforce; provide continuity across time and contractor (so that, for instance, two contractors do not work at cross-purposes); represent training and concept-of-operations (CONOPS) issues that the FAA must face; and provide crucial input to key acquisition decisions. Although some of these issues can be specified by a program office in a contract, some of the human factors consequences are revealed only by experts, HITLS, and so on.

---

[5] T.B. Sheridan, Human response is lognormal; plan on waiting if you want reliability, *Ergonomics in Design* 21(1):4-6, 2013.

## Implications for Operations and Procedures

The medium-term plan will not fundamentally change the roles and activities of pilots and controllers. However, even with modest changes, experience shows that if the result is multiple (modest) changes to systems from what people are accustomed, misunderstandings and errors can result.

Looking ahead, the implications for operations and procedures of NextGen's long-term goals and associated technical changes could be significant. Thus, procedure redesign and airspace design can become a large bottleneck to making progress. The 2013 Implementation Plan[6] provides a nice summary of the FAA vision (at that point) of how things would eventually work gate-to-gate. That discussion makes clear that there are many new systems, all being developed under different programs and at different stages of implementation, being tested at different airports and coming online at different times. The timing of the implementation of the various elements complicates the human factors challenges. Within actual flight operations, there has been little opportunity as yet to observe interactions between the many new systems and procedures, since few airlines are equipped with required avionics beyond what exists a priori within the flight management systems. Further, a key assertion being made by proponents of "resilience engineering," with which the committee concurs, is that errors and failures tend to occur when changes are introduced in systems, and the more simultaneous the changes, the greater the risks.

Some of the anticipated automation in NextGen will likely result in challenging and (at least initially) error-prone new tasks for controllers and pilots. Although automation is expected to provide benefits over the long term, major new tasks for pilots and controllers that merit close attention to procedure design, airspace design, and human factors include the following:

- Automation of navigation based on Global Positioning System and many new navigation aids, especially for arrivals but also including navigation around weather cells and surface movements. New computer-based decision aids are bound to make controllers more dependent on the computer advice given. How is that expected to affect policies for assigning authority and responsibility? New thinking is required beyond the naïve assumptions that the human operators must always be in charge. If computers can recognize invalid input, improper action and/or inattention, under what circumstances should the automation take over control

---

[6] Federal Aviation Administration (FAA), *NextGen Implementation Plan*, Washington, D.C., June 2013.

from the human controller? One could imagine a mechanism for rapid shifting of decision-making roles in off-nominal situations.

- A change from primarily voice to data for air-ground communication. This transition will inevitably create new opportunities for human error (for example, misreading of text input).
- New automation for anticipating and resolving aircraft conflicts, which is supposed to relieve controllers of having to stare at screens to vector aircraft moment to moment, enabling them to take on more planning functions, and enable flow controllers to anticipate traffic flow congestion around airports well upstream.
- A new need for both controllers and pilots to think in time differences as well as spatial geometry—which can get confusing.
- Greater demand than in the current air traffic control (ATC) system for real-time coordination between sector controllers, flow controllers, tower controllers, and pilots for some aspects of NextGen. For example, where controllers used to be responsible for only what was in their own sector, there is an effort is to get them to anticipate upstream and downstream activity more broadly by using new weather and traffic decision support tools. What means are being used to ensure that all parties to the cooperation are seeing the same picture?

Ultimately, realizing any intended benefits to the NAS from improved operations and procedures will require pursuing and completing operational integration. The committee learned that required navigation performance (RNP) and area navigation (RNAV) routes and procedures often go unexploited. Even if aircraft are equipped and pilots are trained, insufficient RNP/RNAV routes have been designed to make a significant difference in the overall performance of the NAS, and there seems little incentive for approach controllers to issue them to arriving aircraft that are properly equipped.[7] This will require funding and commitment to see these things through. Funding development of new capabilities—many of them quite promising—and then curtailing deployment to economize on the backend is not prudent.

---

[7] A detailed examination of the RNP approach at Midway airport with Southwest Airlines (SWA) equipage found that the system-wide fuel savings did not justify the equipment costs to SWA in and of itself. The benefits were more to other airlines operating out of O'Hare airport due to complex airport airspace interactions. See Akshay Belle, "A Methodology for Analysis of Metroplex Air Traffic Flows" Ph.D. dissertation, George Mason University, November 2013. Also see A. Belle, M. Wambsganss, and L. Sherry, "A Methodology for Airport Arrival Flow Analysis Using Track Data—A Case study for MDW Arrivals," *Integrated Communications, Navigation and Surveillance Conference (ICNS), 2013*, 2013, http://ieeexplore.ieee.org/xpls/abs_all.jsp?arnumber=6548547&tag=1.

## A Living CONOPS

Early in the NextGen development, the FAA put out a CONOPS with some useful detail on the expected new roles of pilots and controllers.[8] Since then, however, it has not been updated frequently, and what is available now does not seem to be aligned with the changes that have taken place in NextGen over time. The Implementation Plan has details about programs and includes flight operations in a very general sense, but has very little substance on operations from the pilot and controller perspectives. The 2007 NRC report *Human-System Integration in the System Development Process*[9] emphasized the importance of a frequently updated visualization of the whole system design with off-ramp references to detailed working papers, and so on. This could be thought of as an updated working CONOPS, just as the system architecture should be thought of as a living architecture (and not static descriptions of systems after major decisions have been made). The CONOPS that was issued was perhaps useful to audiences outside of the FAA and NextGen, but not as helpful to system developers or others situated within stovepipes; it has likely resulted in inappropriate expectations about NextGen that persist today. A living CONOPS is related to the system architecture ideas discussed earlier. Both allow for clear, high-level exposition of NextGen and NAS properties that is kept up to date and that informs all stakeholders about the continuing evolution of the NAS. Although they are two distinct perspectives, both are useful.

> **Finding: Numerous constraints challenge the ability of the FAA to smoothly and effectively make changes to its systems and procedures. Human factors for crew and controllers are important to successful changes. Procedures and airspace redesign go hand-in-hand with technical changes and are often just as complicated—and thus a bottleneck to realizing expected benefits of new technologies and approaches.**
>
> **Recommendation: The Federal Aviation Administration (FAA) should recognize and incorporate in early design phases the human factors and procedural and airspace implications of stated goals and associated technical changes. In addition, the FAA should ensure that a human factors specialist, separate from the research and certi-**

---

[8] Joint Planning and Development Office, *Concept of Operations for the Next Generation Air Transportation System*, Version 3.2, http://www.dtic.mil/dtic/tr/fulltext/u2/a535795.pdf.

[9] NRC, *Human-System Integration in the System Development Process: A New Look*, The National Academies Press, Washington, D.C., 2007.

fication groups, have sign-off authority within the Next Generation Air Transportation System approval process.

## COSTS AND BENEFITS

The NAS is a national infrastructure to which significant resources are devoted. As such, it has numerous stakeholders, and there are few individuals or businesses in the country that do not have an interest in or expectations regarding its performance. Thus, the NAS, the FAA, and NextGen efforts are subject to significant scrutiny—not only from users (such as trade groups, airlines, airports, and affiliated labor groups), but from Congress, other federal agencies, and the flying public as well. And as a federal agency, the FAA must operate within the federal political environment and under whatever financial and performance constraints and expectations are produced within it.

The FAA lays out a business case for NextGen in *The Business Case for the Next Generation Air Transportation System: FY 2013*.[10] The committee held several discussions with FAA staff as well to understand the analysis used to develop the costs and benefits of implementing NextGen. In summary, the FAA suggests that NextGen midterm improvements will generate $182 billion in benefits through 2020 and cost approximately $39 billion.

NextGen's benefits are expected to accrue to stakeholders; however, many of those benefits cannot be fully realized without participation and (sometimes costly) adoption by the relevant stakeholders.[11] Nor is there a well-specified overview of what is and is not known about the value of various proposed levels of change (e.g., partial deployment of certain technologies or features). The architecture leadership community has a role to play with respect to managing system-level trade-offs and how they bear on cost and schedule, as discussed in Chapter 2.

Although many of the NextGen advances should benefit participants in the NAS writ large, the fact that some of the benefits may accrue to competitors could be a disincentive to participation by private entities. Thus, for some NextGen goals, the FAA is caught in a bind due to the distributed costs of deployment and the uncertainty of those costs if broad deployment does not occur. The expectation that economic benefits will sufficiently motivate airline equipment purchases may be misplaced, calling into question whether the anticipated voluntary uptake will occur.

---

[10] FAA, *The Business Case for the Next Generation Air Transportation System: FY 2013*, Washington, D.C., 2013.

[11] For example, ADS-B must be installed not only in larger commercial aircraft but also in smaller general aviation aircraft to make full use of the system everywhere and there are costs (financial and also process) associated with deploying this technology.

NextGen plans require a substantial investment, both by the taxpayer via the FAA for infrastructure and by carriers and aircraft owners for equipage and training. At best, benefits—however quantified—to carriers will lag deployment costs, and benefits that accrue to the carriers will be less than the projected social benefits to the system as a whole. Whether something is cost beneficial to a specific entity (FAA, the airlines as a group, a specific airline, or general aviation) can vary greatly and poses a major challenge for NextGen equipage, implementation, training, and so on. Moreover, the required spending is in real dollars, while nearly two-thirds of the economic social benefit is quantified in the form of reduced delays to passengers, as is standard for Department of Transportation analyses of this sort.[12] The FAA does incorporate some savings in aircraft operations in its benefits total, but most of the anticipated benefits stem from estimated costs of passenger time and environmental and safety benefits;[13] the passenger delay reduction accounts for $107 billion of the expected benefits.

The FAA does not fully control NextGen; many of the participants have to actively choose to acquire elements and participate. Voluntary systems are much more likely to succeed when the preferred configuration is locally preferred for each participant, and not just globally preferred on a cost-benefit basis. But, as outlined above, many of the benefits may be socially accrued, resulting in a cost-benefit equation may not actually be positive for many of the required decision makers. In addition, carriers typically expect a return on investment of less than 3 years, whereas the FAA's development cycle can be much longer. These issues constitute a major risk. However, the solution to this problem is not necessarily technical. It may be that it would be best addressed by policy changes or other approaches, which are beyond the scope of this report.

Many of the benefits of NextGen cannot be meaningfully realized unless all, or nearly all, air carriers equip their fleets with the requisite technology.[14] The carriers will also incur training costs, both for new equipage and for new procedures that use old equipage. For airlines to gain significant benefit, NextGen capabilities will need to be deployed at

---

[12] Polly Trottenberg, U.S. Department of Transportation, memorandum to Secretarial Officers and Modal Administrators, "Revised Departmental Guidance on Valuation of Travel Time in Economic Analysis," September 28, 2011, http://www.dot.gov/sites/dot.dev/files/docs/vot_guidance_092811c.pdf.

[13] The passenger value time is based on Department of Transportation guidance from 2011 and is $43.50 per hour, with a 1.6 percent growth per year. Quantifying environmental and safety impacts is also difficult and the methodology can found in the FAA's report *The Business Case for the Next Generation Air Transportation System* (2013).

[14] General aviation faces cost challenges as well, especially related to ADS-B Out avionics, which are still quite expensive compared to other operating and capital costs.

sufficient scale, and given the delay in implementing new procedures and technologies at major airports, airlines may not see benefits for some time. Some of the benefits from new technologies and associated procedures will not be realized until the system is operating at scale. However, some of the demand and capacity pressure present when NextGen was first envisaged have been reduced, which has reduced the urgency for achieving some of the anticipated benefits. In addition, the FAA's current analysis does not take into account potentially negative costs related to possible security breaches absent improvements—a difficult thing to quantify, to be sure, but consideration of these sorts of aspects could be illuminating. Particular NextGen technologies and likely cost-benefit implications of each are discussed below.

- *ADS-B Out.* There is a mandate in place that will require ADS-B Out equipment by January 1, 2020, on all aircraft operating in nearly all NAS Controlled Airspace.[15] The costs of the equipage must be borne by the operators, but the benefits mostly accrue to the FAA in the form of streamlined ATC procedures and information and (theoretically, at least) the retirement of some old and costly surveillance radar. This, of course, requires the mandate, because all aircraft have to be similarly equipped.
- *ADS-B In.* This capability, when available, could provide significant benefits to the aircraft, including much improved situational awareness, predictive traffic information, and delegated separation. Unfortunately, there is no technical specification for these details and no schedule for a mandated implementation to drive the development of one. Moreover, achieving some of these benefits will require changes in software and controller procedures. Without a credible implementation schedule, carriers will discount or dismiss the value of these capabilities.
- *Performance-based navigation (PBN).* Almost all Part 121 (Air Carrier) aircraft are equipped with some level of highly capable RNP, as are many general aviation aircraft. But use of these procedures at airports remains low.[16] The problem with extracting associated benefits from the use of PBN is the absence of necessary procedure design by the FAA. In order to demonstrate progress some years ago, many existing procedures using ground-based navigational aids were simply converted using identical trajectories that simply overlay GPS waypoints. New procedures are required that truly utilize the precision of a modern flight management

---

[15] FAA, "Automatic Dependent Surveillance-Broadcast Operations," Advisory Circular, October 28, 2014, http://www.faa.gov/documentLibrary/media/Advisory_Circular/AC_90-114A_FAA_Web_%282%29.pdf.

[16] Matthew Hampton, Assistant IG for Aviation Audits, memorandum, "Audit Announcement—FAA Progress in Deploying Controller Automation Tools for Performance-Based Navigation Flight Procedures," July 1, 2014.

system in terminal procedures and in parallel-track en route navigation. The community has already invested heavily in this underutilized equipment, which makes them reluctant to rely on FAA schedules or commitments regarding other efforts.

- *Other NextGen capabilities*, like Data Communications (Data Comm) and Digital Voice, eventually will yield some efficiencies and reduce some human error but the emphasis has been on technology, not on quantified benefits. Although the FAA offers some modest incentives for Data Comm equipage, in general, there is little incentive for carriers to implement early and participate in a redesign of the airspace, which should be accompanying all this new technology. Instead, much of the airspace remains in the configurations established 50 years ago by the constraints of ground-based radio frequency navigational aids.

> **Finding:** The costs and benefits analysis presented to the committee was sensible; however, an ongoing challenge for the FAA and Congress is that most of the benefits accrue to the public at large—largely in the form of reductions in delays—while costs are borne by others, such as the carriers.

> **Finding:** Current short- and medium-term goals for NextGen emphasize new technologies to improve and enhance existing capabilities. Although modernization efforts are important and can bring significant benefits, it is a challenge to incentivize uptake for equipage, training, or changes in procedures absent clear benefits.

> **Recommendation:** Preceding any further equipage mandate, the Federal Aviation Administration (FAA) should provide an estimated statement of costs and benefits that is mutually reviewed and agreed upon with the relevant stakeholders. It should be based on a mature and stable technical specification and a committed timeline for FAA deliverables and investment (for procedure and airspace design, infrastructure deployment, training, and so on). On this basis, industry could responsibly invest as required, given a reasonable expected return.

## THE CHALLENGE OF BEING A SYSTEM INTEGRATOR

The FAA does not operate in a vacuum. When it comes to large government systems and software projects, it faces many of the same challenges as many other government agencies, among them are the following: a reliance on waterfall approaches to software development, difficulty in hiring and retaining skilled information technology (IT) professionals, policies and requirements developed without sufficient technical or engineering input, and acquisition and budgeting processes not designed for the way modern software systems are built.[17]

The problems with air traffic control and airspace modernization, in the face of rapid technology change and challenging governmental budgeting requirements, have not been unique to the United States. Most modern industrialized countries have experienced the same problems. Most noticeable and relevant to the U.S. system are the Canadian, British, German, and Australian systems. Each has proceeded in its own way to separate the (mostly industrial) function of air traffic control from the essential governmental oversight function and responsibility that is demanded of sovereign nations under the Chicago Convention Treaty of 1944.[18] The managerial and technical expertise required to constantly upgrade modern telecommunications systems is challenging for any government agency to attract and maintain. In addition, culturally, most government employees are risk averse and conservative in action due to the high level of public accountability and close oversight intrinsic to any government operation. This is not an environment in which most highly skilled engineers choose to be employed.[19]

Most NextGen software development is outsourced to contractors, thus obliging the FAA to act as the system integrator. However, the FAA's NextGen team is ill-equipped—in terms of having sufficient broad and deep expertise and in terms of resources—to perform as a system integrator. Without sufficient system architecture competence and mature architectural approaches, the probability of success is compromised. Of particular note, the committee did not hear much from the FAA or its contractors about change management—especially in the case of important changes required by the agency rather than those managed entirely within the contractor's own software and system development processes.

Second, the committee has a concern about the criteria being used to evaluate and assess software contractors. In briefings to the committee, there was significant emphasis placed on contractor software development maturity (e.g., capability maturity model integration, or CMMI) and less emphasis on contractor track record for value delivery. Federal procurements use a "best value" criterion above all others with strong

---

[17] For more information about transforming large-scale government acquisition of software-intensive systems in a more agile manner, see NRC, *Achieving Effective Acquisition of Information Technology in the Department of Defense*, The National Academies Press, Washington, D.C., 2010.

[18] The Convention on International Civil Aviation was signed on December 7, 1944, and is available at http://www.icao.int/publications/Documents/7300_orig.pdf.

[19] Due to the nature of the challenges, threats, and incentives, the Department of Defense may be a possible exception to this observation.

emphasis on past performance. One element may be a CMMI rating, but that is one of many factors.[20] However, like the risk management process, the software and the acquisition approaches seem to be overly process driven, not outcome driven. The committee's impression is that there was little apparent concern for increased efficiency that can be channeled into cost reduction, timeliness improvement, or quality improvement. While high ratings for capability maturity are desirable, they do not sufficiently reflect the quality of products delivered, or the effectiveness of the contractor in exploiting software to leverage existing capabilities, or exploit emerging technologies to best effect. At the same time, contractor efforts to work collaboratively with others on better integration are undoubtedly hampered by stovepiping and procurement regulations.

If the FAA is to succeed in both the medium and long term, it will require enhancements to its technical expertise. Architecture and systems engineering, which are needed for successful integration of capabilities and platforms into a coherent NAS system, have been undervalued. Program management and systems engineering process are important but are not a substitute for talent that can effectively guide the design and evolution of NextGen. This is especially important if the FAA continues to act as the systems integrator of NextGen programs. In that role, the FAA should maintain architectural leadership and not delegate architecture definition and control to contractors.

Today, the FAA relies greatly on its vendors and other external talent. Internally, the FAA depends on a very small number of individuals and lacks the critical mass that characterizes a vibrant and effective technical community. Digital communications will take on increasing importance as the NAS is modernized, so the FAA will need additional technical expertise in designing modern digital networks and protocols. Historically, air traffic control has relied heavily on analog voice communications, but with programs like Data Comm, digital communication will increasingly become primary. Cybersecurity is a challenge facing all who use modern computing and communications technology, and the potential threats and risks are magnified for critical infrastructure, like the systems that make

---

[20] Indeed, government contractors generally (beyond FAA contractors) have been required to complete CMMI assessments since the 1990s, but government software acquisition programs continue to suffer from delayed schedules and inadequate product performance. A 2014 GAO report on information technology reform initiatives noted that "federal IT projects too frequently fail and incur cost overruns and schedule slippages while contributing little to mission-related outcomes" (GAO, *Information Technology: Reform Initiatives Can Help Improve Efficiency and Effectiveness*, Statement of David A. Powner, Director, Information Technology Management Issues, Testimony Before the Subcommittee on Efficiency and Effectiveness of Federal Programs and the Federal Workforce, Committee on Homeland Security and Governmental Affairs, U.S. Senate, http://www.gao.gov/products/GAO-14-671T).

up the NAS. The FAA needs strong cybersecurity expertise in designing, implementing, integrating, and operating NextGen systems. Finally, while the FAA should emphasize organic talent, it will also be fruitful in today's world for the FAA to regularly tap into outside communities of expertise. Even if the FAA were not acting as systems integrator, it would still need to be a "smart customer,"—meaning that it needs expertise that will enable it to effectively structure and manage its supplier relationships.

Developing and retaining this expertise will be a challenge. However, proceeding with inexperienced or less than the best personnel in key leadership positions is a significant risk.[21] The FAA will likely need to tap into its "government-side" network of partners in federally funded research and development centers, systems engineering and technical assistance contractors, and similar organizations in order to gain access to sufficient expertise. It will also need to examine the incentive structure it creates for its primes (and into the supply chain as well) to better align incentives around the risk-managed, architecture-led processes above. These incentives can include earned-value models, rewards, and penalties. There also need to be processes for the various NextGen primes (and potentially bidders) to participate in the architecting process in a way that the architectural decisions that emerge will be respected and supported by those involved in program execution (rather than being used as an excuse to incur additional costs).

**Finding: Like other federal agencies, the FAA faces challenges implementing IT systems and in recruiting and retaining the workforce needed for designing, maintaining, and enhancing systems such as NextGen. In particular, the FAA is ill-equipped to perform as a systems integrator.**

**Recommendation: The Federal Aviation Administration (FAA) should nurture workforce talent in the areas of systems engineering, architecture, systems integration, digital communications, and cybersecurity. Significant effort will be required to attract, develop, and retain this talent, given the high demand outside the FAA.**

**Recommendation: Should the Federal Aviation Administration (FAA) continue to act as the systems integrator of Next Generation**

---

[21] From NRC, *Pre-Milestone A and Early-Phase Systems Engineering*, 2008: "Perhaps the biggest risk of all in undertaking large development programs is to proceed with less than the best personnel, particularly in the key leadership positions in government and industry. High-quality program managers and system engineering leaders, in particular, are critical. High aptitude and extensive experience, combining to create high domain knowledge, are required for individuals to be fully effective in these positions" (p. 82).

Air Transportation System programs, it should maintain architectural leadership and not delegate architecture definition and control to contractors.

## SUPPORT FOR OPERATIONS AND MAINTENANCE

A common fallacy with software-intensive systems is that they can be built, deployed, and then operate with relatively little "maintenance" and modernization effort. The surprise, for those unfamiliar with such systems, is that operations and maintenance will very often include substantial modernization effort. This effort is needed both in response to new requirements and also in response to rapid growth and change in technological infrastructure. This is true for NextGen and the NAS, as the rest of this report has described, and this fact has implications for how the FAA should explain its needs to Congress and its overseers.

Congress plays an important and complex role in its relationship with the FAA and NextGen. One facet of its role is oversight, which it has done diligently ever since the formation of the FAA in 1958 and especially since the time of the controllers' strike and the FAA's response and later the Advanced Automation System (AAS) problems. However, in its role of authorization and appropriations, it has increasingly played an indirect role in the management of the FAA and has always acted as its banker. Since the AAS, Congress has passed legislation aimed at improving the FAA's ability to modernize the ATC system.

In the 1996 Appropriations Bill, the FAA was given nearly unique authority to revise its acquisition regulations (FAA's Acquisition Management System is broader and less prescriptive than the Federal Acquisition Regulation) and its personnel system. The aim was to allow the agency to attract the necessary technical personnel and to more rapidly and efficiently acquire the telecommunications equipment, software, and systems integration required of a modern air traffic control system. Some of these reforms were especially useful in the late 1990s and early 2000s. Despite these measures, today's FAA, like many other government agencies, has trouble attracting and retaining sufficient technical talent to support its missions. And in 2004, the community was calling for even better performance and a more bold vision of the future. Congress then approved the formation of the Joint Planning and Development Office (JPDO), allowed for the new position of chief operating officer to be recruited from industry, and reorganized the FAA air traffic control organization, based on an airline industrial model. Congress further authorized the formation of an oversight committee composed of industry and government experts and managers. In spite of these proactive measures on the part of Congress, the FAA's NextGen program is still moving at a pace slower than desired and is now facing the new requirement of accommodating unmanned aircraft systems into civil airspace.

As for any large-scale government IT effort, a long-term commitment is important. Although Congress has been supportive of FAA efforts, as the above discussion makes clear, in the committee's view, there is a specific need for support of ongoing maintenance and modernization (upgrades) and refreshing and modernizing of both hardware and software to provide reliable, cost-effective operation.[22] Too often in government, funds are allocated for specific (new) programs or projects without sufficient allocation for the full life-cycle costs and for maintenance and refresh of existing (and still important) programs.[23]

NextGen is and will be a continuously evolving system-of-systems and should not be thought of as one large monolith. NextGen needs to continually evaluate new technologies and approaches and then make decisions about what to incorporate and how. This means that there will be some reconceptualization going on while there is also a great deal of implementation happening, perhaps of components that are already being scheduled to be phased out. A system architecture, as discussed earlier in the report, is essential, always. But there must be flexibility for the system architecture to evolve, too, with consequent changes down the line leading ultimately to the implementation of a deployed system. In this respect, NextGen needs to be managed and evolved very much like other large systems (e.g., financial systems and retail systems) that are constantly evolving, requiring that management and financing recognize this need for evolvability. A large software-intensive system is not "bought" once and for all, but rather put into place and then continually maintained and evolved at continuing cost and effort.[24] Finally, as discussed in Chapter 1, Congress itself can partner with the FAA in acknowledging the changing context and adjusting expectations as appropriate.

---

[22] Learning from the NavCanada experience would be useful. A financially stable, long-term business model is required to both organize and attract the necessary technical talent/expertise with a dependable income stream to provide project stability and predictability to design and deploy such a complex system.

[23] Lessons from the private sector suggest that there are many other equally significant opportunities for support of such systems, such as continuity and timeliness of funding, color of money, directed funding, addressing the lack of discretionary funds, and more readily moving funds where needed the most. These are common practices in running a corporation that are not typically available within the government structure.

[24] This is increasingly inconsistent with waterfall-style software development approaches that discourage revisiting early concepts and architectures and that can thwart innovation and evolution.

**Finding:** As a large-scale, software-intensive system, NextGen and the NAS will benefit if ongoing maintenance of the NAS and its hardware and software systems are supported—in addition to programmatic investments; such an approach will make the most of past and ongoing investments.

# Appendixes

# A

# Biographies of Committee Members and Staff

DAVID E. LIDDLE, *Chair*, has been a partner at U.S. Venture Partners, a Silicon Valley-based venture capital firm since 2000. He co-founded Interval Research Corporation, a Silicon Valley-based laboratory and incubator for new businesses focusing on broadband, consumer devices, interaction design, and advanced technologies, where he served as president and CEO between 1992 and 1999. Previously, Dr. Liddle co-founded Metaphor Computer Systems, Inc., in 1982 and served as its president and CEO until 1991. He has also held executive positions at Xerox Corporation and IBM. Prior to co-founding Interval with Paul Allen, Dr. Liddle founded Metaphor, which was acquired by IBM in 1991, which named him vice president of business development for IBM Personal Systems. His extensive experience in research and development has focused largely on human-computer interactions and includes 10 years at Xerox Palo Alto Research Center (PARC), from 1972 to 1982. He has been a director of MaxLinear, Sybase, Broderbund Software, Borland International, and Ticketmaster and is currently on the board of the New York Times Company and InPhi, Inc. His board involvement at U.S. Venture Partners includes AltoBeam, Karmasphere, and LineStream. Dr. Liddle served on the Defense Advanced Research Projects Agency (DARPA) Information Science and Technology Committee and as co-chair of the National Research Council's (NRC's) Computer Science and Telecommunications board. His contributions to human-computer interaction design earned him the distinction of senior fellow at the Royal College of Art. He is on the boards of SRI International, the College of Engineering at Stanford

University and The Public Library of Science. Dr, Liddle earned a B.S. in electrical engineering at the University of Michigan and a Ph.D. in EECS at the University of Toledo, where his dissertation focused on reconfigurable computing machines and theories of encryption, encoding, and signal recovery. He recently served as chair of the NRC study on wireless technology prospects and policy options, and on the subsequent PCAST study on realizing the full potential of government-held spectrum to spur economic growth. He is a type-rated Citation pilot with more than 2,000 hours in jets.

STEVEN M. BELLOVIN is the Percy K. and Vidal L. W. Hudson Professor of Computer Science at Columbia University, where he does research on networks, security, and especially why the two do not get along. He recently served as the chief technologist for the Federal Trade Commission. He joined the faculty at Columbia in 2005 after many years at Bell Labs and AT&T Labs Research where he was an AT&T fellow. He received a B.A. degree from Columbia University and his M.S. and Ph.D. degrees in computer science from the University of North Carolina, Chapel Hill. While a graduate student, he helped create Netnews; for this, he and the other perpetrators were given the 1995 Usenix Lifetime Achievement Award (The Flame). In 2007 he received the National Institute of Standards and Technology/National Security Agency National Computer Systems Security Award. He is a member of the National Academy of Engineering (NAE) and is serving on the Department of Homeland Security's Science and Technology Advisory Committee and the Technical Guidelines Development Committee of the Election Assistance Commission. He was a member of the Internet Architecture Board from 1996-2002 and was co-director of the Security Area of the Internet Engineering Task Forcefrom 2002 through 2004. Dr. Bellovin is the co-author of *Firewalls and Internet Security: Repelling the Wily Hacker,* and holds a number of patents on cryptographic and network protocols. He has served on many NRC committees, including those on information systems trustworthiness, the privacy implications of authentication technologies, and cybersecurity research needs. He was also a member of the information technology subcommittee of an NRC study group on science versus terrorism.

JOHN-PAUL B. CLARKE is an associate professor in the Daniel Guggenheim School of Aerospace Engineering with a courtesy appointment in the H. Milton Stewart School of Industrial and Systems Engineering and director of the Air Transportation Laboratory at the Georgia Institute of Technology. He received S.B., S.M. , and Sc.D. degrees in aeronautics and astronautics from the Massachusetts Institute of Technology (MIT). His research and teaching in the areas of control, optimization, and system analysis, architecture, and design are motivated by his desire to simultaneously maximize the efficiency and minimize the societal costs (especially on the environment) of the global air transportation system. Dr. Clarke has made seminal contributions in the areas of air traffic management, aircraft operations, and airline operations—the three key elements of the air transportation system—and has been recognized globally for developing, among other things, key analytical foundations for the Continuous Descent Arrival and novel concepts for robust airline scheduling. His research has resulted in significant changes in engineering methods, processes, and products—most notably the development of new arrival procedures for four major U.S. airports and one European airport—and changes in airline scheduling practices. He is an associate fellow of the American Institute of Aeronautics and Astronautics (AIAA) and a member of the Airline Group of the International Federation of Operational Research Societies, Institute for Operations Research and the Management Sciences, and Sigma Xi. His many honors include the AIAA/AAAE/ACC Jay Hollingsworth Speas Airport Award (1999), the Federal Aviation Administration (FAA) Excellence in Aviation Award (2003), the NAE Gilbreth Lecturership (2006), and the 37th SAE/AIAA William Littlewood Memorial Lecture Award (2012).

GEORGE L. DONOHUE was granted the status of professor emeritus in 2010 and has been a professor of systems engineering and operations research at George Mason University since 2000. He has an M.S. and a Ph.D. in mechanical and aerospace engineering from Oklahoma State University and a BSME from the University of Houston. From 1994 to 1998, he was the associate administrator for research and acquisitions at the FAA and is the founding director of the Center for Air Transportation Systems Research in the Volgenau School of Engineering. Dr. Donohue is a former vice president of the RAND Corporation and director of PROJECT AIR FORCE (1989-1994). Previously he was the director of DARPA's Aerospace and Strategic Technology Office (1988-1989), a vice president of Dynamics Technology (1979-1984). He served as head of the Advanced Technology Division (1977-1979) and head of the Fluid Mechanics Branch (1973-1976) at the U.S. Naval Ocean System Center in San Diego, California. In the interim, he served as a program manager in DARPA's Tactical Technology Office (1976-1977). He has been awarded an NRC post-doctoral fellowship with the U.S. Navy (1973-1974), the Secretary of Defense Meritorious Civilian Service Medal (1977), the Air Traffic Control Association Clifford Burton Memorial Award (1998), and the Embry Riddle Aeronautical University Pinnacle Award for initiating the Alaska Capstone ADS-B Program (2007). He was named one of *Federal Computer Week's* top 100 Executives in 1997 and was also named one of the top 100 decision makers in Washington, D.C., by the *National Journal* in 1997. Dr. Donohue was chosen to head the U.S. Delegation to the International Civil Aviation Organization-Conference on Air Traffic Management Modernization in 1998. He is a member of Tau Beta Pi, Pi Tau Sigma, Omicron Delta Kappa, and Sigma Xi honorary societies. He is a fellow of AIAA and a licensed private pilot with a single-engine land rating. In addition to more than 60 published unclassified papers, he has been the principal author of two books on air transportation, the most recent is titled *Terminal Chaos: Why U.S. Air Travel is Broken and How to Fix It*. He has testified before Congress on both military and civil aviation issues on numerous occasions. Dr. Donohue is currently acting as an academic advisor to undergraduate and doctoral students. He is a member of the NRC's NASA Aeronautics Research and Technology Roundtable, and a member of the Mechanical and Aerospace Engineering Advisory Board, Oklahoma State University.

R. JOHN HANSMAN, JR. is the T. Wilson Professor in the Department of Aeronautics and Astronautics at MIT, where he is head of the Humans and Automation Division. He also is director of the International Center for Air Transportation. His current research interests focus on advanced cockpit information systems, including flight management systems, air-ground datalink, electronic charting, advanced alerting systems, and flight crew situational awareness. Dr. Hansman received a Ph.D. from MIT. He holds six U.S. Patents and has authored more than 250 technical publications. He is also an internationally recognized expert in aviation meteorological hazards such as icing and windshear. He is a member of the NAE and a fellow of AIAA. He received the 1998 Bose Award for Excellence in Teaching, the 1997 FAA Excellence in Aviation Award, the 1994 AIAA Losey Atmospheric Award, the 1990 OSTIV Diploma for Technical Contributions, and the 1986 AIAA Award for Best Paper in Thermophysics. He recently served as co-chair of the MIT Presidential Task Force on Student Life and Learning. Dr. Hansman consults and serves as a member of numerous advisory and technical committees, including the Congressional Aeronautics Advisory Committee, the FAA Research and Development Advisory Committee, the FAA WAAS Independent Review Board, and the NASA Advanced Air Transportation Technologies Executive Steering Committee. He serves on several editorial boards, including *Air Traffic Control Quarterly*. He has more than 5,650 hours of pilot in-command time in airplanes, helicopters, and sailplanes, including meteorological, production, and engineering flight test experience.

MATS P.E. HEIMDAHL is the director of the University of Minnesota Software Engineering Center where he specializes in software engineering and safety critical systems. Dr. Heimdahl is the recipient of the National Science Foundation's CAREER award and University of Minnesota's McKnight

Land-Grant Professorship, the McKnight Presidential Fellow Award, and the Award for Outstanding Contributions to Post-Baccalaureate, Graduate, and Professional Education. His research group, the Critical Systems Research Group, is conducting research in software engineering and is investigating methods and tools to help develop software with predictable behavior free from defects. Research in this area spans all aspects of system development ranging from concept formation and requirements specification through design and implementation to testing and maintenance. In particular, he is investigating model-based software development for critical systems, focusing on how to use various static verification techniques to assure that software requirements models possess desirable properties, how to correctly generate production code from software requirements models, how to validate models, and how to effectively use the models in the testing process.

JOHN C. KNIGHT is a professor of computer science at the University of Virginia. He holds a B.Sc. (Hons) in mathematics from the Imperial College of Science and Technology (London) and a Ph.D. in computer science from the University of Newcastle upon Tyne. Prior to joining the University of Virginia in 1981, he was with NASA's Langley Research Center. He was the general chair of the 2000 International Symposium on the Foundations of Software Engineering (FSE), and general chair of the 2007 International Conference on Software Engineering (ICSE). He served as editor in chief of *IEEE Transactions on Software Engineering* from January 2002 to December 2005. He was honored by the IEEE Computer Society as the recipient of the 2006 Harlan D. Mills Award "for encouraging software researchers to focus on practical results as well as theory, and for critically analyzing their assumptions and evaluating their research claims." He was honored by the Association for Computing Machinery's (ACM's) Special Interest Group on Software Engineering (SIGSOFT) as the recipient of the 2008 Distinguished Service Award.

LEON J. OSTERWEIL is a professor in the Department of Computer Science and co-director of the Laboratory for Advanced Software Engineering Research at the University of Massachusetts, Amherst. He served as dean of the College of Natural Sciences and Mathematics at the University of Massachusetts, as chair of the Information and Computer Science Department of the University of California, Irvine, and chair of the Computer Science Department at the University of Colorado, Boulder. Dr. Osterweil received the Outstanding Research Award for lifetime achievement in research and the Influential Educator Award, both from ACM SIGSOFT. His paper suggesting the idea of process programming was recognized as the Most Influential Paper of the 9th International Conference on Software

Engineering, awarded as a 10-year retrospective. Dr. Osterweil has served on the editorial boards of several journals, including *IEEE Software, IEEE Transactions on Software Engineering,* and *ACM Transactions on Software Engineering and Methodology.* He has served as program chair for many conferences, including the 16th ICSE, and as general chair of the 28th ICSE and the 6th FSE. He was a member of the Software Engineering Institute's Process Program Advisory Board for several years following its inception and has been an advisor or consultant for such organizations as SAIC, MCC, AT&T, Boeing, KLA-Tencor, TRW, and IBM. He has been a keynote speaker at many conferences around the world. Dr. Osterweil is a fellow of the ACM and an ACM Lecturer.

WALKER E. ROYCE is the chief software economist in IBM Software Group. He is a principal consultant and practice leader specializing in measured improvement of systems and software development capability. He is the author of three books: *Eureka! Discover and Enjoy the Hidden Power of the English Language* (2011), *The Economics of Software Development* (2009) and *Software Project Management, A Unified Framework* (1998). From 1994-2009, Mr. Royce was the vice president and general manager of IBM's Rational Services organization and built a worldwide team of 500 technical specialists in software delivery best practices and $100 million in consulting services. Before joining Rational/IBM, he spent 16 years in software project development, software technology development, and software management roles at TRW Electronics and Defense. Mr. Royce was a recipient of TRW's Chairman's Award for Innovation for his contributions in distributed architecture middleware and iterative software processes (1990) and was a TRW technical fellow. He received his B.A. in physics from the University of California and his M.S. in computer engineering from the University of Michigan.

GAVRIEL SALVENDY is professor emeritus of industrial engineering at Purdue University and chair professor emeritus and former head (2001-2011) of the Department of Industrial Engineering at Tsinghua University, Beijing, and P.R. of China. He is the author or co-author of more than 550 research publications, including more than 300 journal papers, and he is the author or editor of 42 books. His publications have appeared in seven languages. He is the major professor to 67 former and current Ph.D. students. His main research deals with the human aspects of design, operation, and management of advanced engineering systems. Dr. Salvendy is the founding editor of *International Journal on Human-Computer Interaction* and *Human Factors and Ergonomics in Manufacturing and Service Industries.* He was the founding chair of the International Commission on Human Aspects in Computing, headquartered in Geneva, Switzerland. In 1990, he became the first member of either the Human Factors and Ergonomics Society or the International Ergonomics Association to be elected to the NAE. He was elected "for fundamental contributions to and professional leadership in human, physical, and cognitive aspects of engineering systems." In 1995, he received an honorary doctorate from the Chinese Academy of Sciences "for great contributions to the development of science and technology and for the great influence upon the development of science and technology in China" and is the fourth person in all fields of science and engineering in the 45 years of the Academy ever to receive this award. In 2006, he received the Friendship Award presented by the People's Republic of China—the highest honor the Chinese government confers on foreign experts. In 2007, he received the John Fritz Medal, which is the engineering profession's highest award, for his "fundamental international and seminal leadership and technical contributions to human engineering and industrial engineering education, theory, and practice." The journals *Ergonomics* (2003), *Computers in Industry* (2010), and *Intelligent Manufacturing* (2011) have published special issues in his honor. He is an honorary fellow and life member of the Ergonomics Society and a fellow of the Human Factors and Ergonomics Society, the Institute of Industrial Engineers, and the American Psychological Association. He has advised organizations in more than 31 countries on the human side of effective design, implementation, and management of advanced technologies in the workplace. He earned his Ph.D. in engineering production at the University of Birmingham, United Kingdom.

THOMAS B. SHERIDAN is the Ford Professor of Engineering and Applied Psychology, Emeritus, in the Department of Mechanical Engineering and the Department of Aeronautics and Astronautics at MIT, where he has spent most of his professional career serving as director of the Human-Machine Systems Laboratory. Dr. Sheridan's research interests are in experimentation, mathematical modeling, and design of human-machine systems in air, highway, and rail transportation, space and undersea robotics, process control, arms control, telemedicine, and virtual reality. He has authored and edited numerous books, co-founded the MIT Press journal *Presence: Teleoperators and Virtual Environments* and served on several editorial boards. Dr. Sheridan chaired and continues to serve on the NRC's Committee on Human Systems Integration and has served on numerous government and industrial advisory committees. Since retiring from MIT, he has served the U.S. government as a senior research fellow for the U.S. Department of Transportation Volpe Center and as chief system engineer for human factors for the FAA. He is a fellow of the Human Factors and Ergonomics Society and a recipient of their Paul M. Fitts and Arnold Small Awards and the President's Outstanding

Career Award, as well as a former president of the society. He was elected to the NAE in 1995. Dr. Sheridan holds a bachelor's degree from Purdue University, an M.S. degree from the University of California, Los Angeles, and a Sc.D. degree from MIT.

ROBERT F. SPROULL recently retired as vice president and director of Oracle Labs, an applied research group that originated at Sun Microsystems. Since his undergraduate days, Dr. Sproull has been building hardware and software for computer graphics, clipping hardware, an early device-independent graphics package, page description languages, laser printing software, and window systems. He has also been involved in very-large-scale integrated circuit design, especially of asynchronous circuits and systems. Before joining Sun Microsystems in 1990 (acquired by Oracle in 2010), he was a principal with Sutherland, Sproull and Associates, an associate professor at Carnegie Mellon University and a member of Xerox PARC. He is a coauthor with William Newman of the early text *Principles of Interactive Computer Graphics*. He is also an author of the book *Logical Effort*, which deals with designing fast complementary metal-oxide–semiconductor circuits. He is a member of the NAE, a fellow of the American Academy of Arts and Sciences, and has served on the U.S. Air Force Scientific Advisory Board and as a technology partner of Advanced Technology Ventures. He is currently the chair of the NRC's Computer Science and Telecommunications Board, a director of Applied Micro Circuits, Inc., and an adjunct professor of computer science at University of Massachusetts, Amherst. Dr. Sproull received a B.A in physics from Harvard College and an M.S. and Ph.D. in computer science from Stanford University.

JAMES W. STURGES is an independent consultant specializing in program management and systems engineering for very large, complex aerospace and defense systems. He retired in 2009 from Lockheed Martin Corporation where he had been director, engineering processes, and director, mission assurance. Prior to that he was vice president, engineering and total quality, at Loral Air Traffic Control/Lockheed Martin Air Traffic Management, and C3I strategic business area director for Loral Tactical Defense Systems, Arizona. He is an associate fellow and past member of the Standards Executive Council and chair of the Systems Engineering Technical Committee of AIAA and was twice chair of the Corporate Advisory Board for the International Council on Systems Engineering. Early in his career, he was a naval aviator, instrument instructor, and check pilot and was an anti-submarine warfare officer for the U.S. Navy. He has a B.A. from the University of North Carolina and an M.S. and aeronautical engineer degree from the Naval Postgraduate School at Monterey.

ELAINE WEYUKER is an ACM fellow, an IEEE fellow, an AT&T fellow, and NAE member. Dr. Weyuker is currently an independent consultant specializing in software testing, reliability, and metrics, and a visiting scholar at the Center for Discrete Mathematics and Theoretical Computer Science of Rutgers, the State University of New Jersey. She is the author of 170 papers in journals and refereed conference proceedings. Prior to moving to the Research Division of AT&T Labs, she was a professor of the Courant Institute of Mathematical Sciences of New York University, was a faculty member at the City University of New York, a systems engineer at IBM, and a programmer at Texaco. She served as chair of the ACM Women's Council from 2004 to 2012, is a member of the steering committee of the Coalition to Diversify Computing, a member of the Rutgers University Graduate School Advisory Board, and was a member of the board of directors of the Computing Research Association. Dr. Weyuker is or was a member of the editorial boards of *IEEE Transactions on Software Engineering, IEEE Transactions on Dependable and Secure Computing, IEEE Spectrum, the Empirical Software Engineering Journal,* and the *Journal of Systems and Software,* and she was a founding editor of *ACM Transactions of Software Engineering and Methodology.* She was the secretary/treasurer of ACM SIGSOFT and was an ACM national lecturer. Dr. Weyuker received a Ph.D. in computer science from Rutgers University, an M.S.E. from the University of Pennsylvania, and a B.A. in mathematics from the State University of New York, Binghamton.

## STAFF

JON EISENBERG is director of the Computer Science and Telecommunications Board (CSTB). He has also been study director for a diverse body of work, including a series of studies exploring Internet and broadband policy and networking and communications technologies. From 1995 to 1997 he was a AAAS Science, Engineering, and Diplomacy Fellow at the U.S. Agency for International Development, where he worked on technology transfer and information and telecommunications policy issues. Dr. Eisenberg received his Ph.D. in physics from the University of Washington and B.S. in physics with honors from the University of Massachusetts, Amherst.

LYNETTE I. MILLETT is associate director of CSTB and director of the Forum on Cyber Resilience. Ms. Millett has extensive experience as program manager, team leader, analyst, researcher, and writer with specific expertise in information technology policy. She is skilled in working with diverse and expert work groups and since 2000 has been developing, directing, and overseeing NRC studies and teams of national experts examining public policy issues related broadly to information technology, computing, software, and communications. Her portfolio at the NRC includes a suite of studies on computing research, the most recent being 2012's *Computing Research for Sustainability*; several examinations of government information technology and infrastructure needs, such as 2011's *Strategies and Priorities for Information Technology at the Centers for Medicare and Medicaid Services*; and in-depth examinations of privacy, identity and cybersecurity, including 2010's *Biometric Recognition: Challenges and Opportunities*. She has an M.Sc. in computer science from Cornell University, where her work was supported by graduate fellowships from the National Science Foundation and the Intel Corporation; and a B.A. in mathematics and computer science with honors from Colby College.

VIRGINIA BACON TALATI is a program officer for the CSTB of the NRC of the National Academies. She formerly served as a program associate with the Frontiers of Engineering program at the NAE. Prior to her work at the Academies, she served as a senior project assistant in Education Technology at the National School Boards Association. Ms. Bacon Talati has a B.S. in science, technology, and culture from the Georgia Institute of Technology and an M.P.P. from George Mason University, with a focus in science and technology policy.

ERIC WHITAKER was a senior program assistant at CSTB until March 2015. Prior to joining CSTB, he was a realtor with Long and Foster Real Estate, Inc., in the Washington, D.C., metropolitan area. Before that, he spent several years with the Public Broadcasting Service in Alexandria, Virginia, as an associate in the Corporate Support Department. He has a B.A. in communication and theater arts from Hampton University.

# B

# Briefers to the Study Committee

Sherry Borener, Federal Aviation Administration
Steven Bradford, Federal Aviation Administration
Edgar Calderon, Federal Aviation Administration
Vincent Capezzuto, Federal Aviation Administration
Rachel Carr, House Aviation Subcommittee, Minority Staff
Sean Cassidy, Air Line Pilot Association
Stephen Dickson, Delta Air Lines
Gerald Dillingham, Government Accountability Office
Glen Dyer, Excelis
Paul Fountain, Federal Aviation Administration
Giles Giovinazzi, House Aviation Subcommittee, Minority Staff
Fran Hill, Lockheed Martin
Michael Hritz, Federal Aviation Administration
Margaret Jenny, RTCA
Charles Keegan, Raytheon
Tom Kramer, Aircraft Owners and Pilots Association
Heather Krause, Government Accountability Office
Paul Krois, Federal Aviation Administration
Andrew Lacher, MITRE
Molly Laster, Government Accountability Office
Natesh Manikoth, Federal Aviation Administration
Mike Matousek, House Aviation Subcommittee, Majority Staff
Jay Merkle, Federal Aviation Administration
Michele Merkle, Federal Aviation Administration

Robert Nichols, Federal Aviation Administration
Roberto Ortiz, Federal Aviation Administration
Madhav Panwar, Government Accountability Office
Simone Perez, House Aviation Subcommittee, Majority Staff
Joseph Post, Federal Aviation Administration
Andrew Rademaker, House Aviation Subcommittee, Majority Staff
Mike Riso, Professional Aviation Safety Specialists
Ron Stroup, Federal Aviation Administration
Rich Swayze, Senate Commerce Committee, Majority Staff
Joseph Teixeira, Federal Aviation Administration
Karlin Toner, Joint Planning and Development Office
Dan Watts, Federal Aviation Administration
Pamela Whitley, Federal Aviation Administration
Jesse Wijntjes, Federal Aviation Administration
Holly Woodruff Lyons, House Aviation Subcommittee, Majority Staff
Dale Wright, National Air Traffic Controllers Association

# C

# Acronyms

| | |
|---|---|
| 4-D | four dimension (time as the 4th dimension) |
| | |
| AAS | Advanced Automation System |
| ADS-B | Automatic Dependent Surveillance-Broadcast |
| ADS-R | Automatic Dependent Surveillance-Rebroadcast |
| AMS | acquisition management system |
| ASSC | Airport Surface Surveillance Capability |
| ATC | air traffic control |
| | |
| CMMI | capability maturity model integration |
| CONOPS | concept of operations |
| | |
| DoDAF | Department of Defense Architecture Framework |
| DOT | Department of Transportation |
| | |
| EGPWS | enhanced ground proximity warning system |
| ERAM | En Route Automation Modernization |
| | |
| FAA | Federal Aviation Administration |
| FAR | Federal Acquisition Regulation |
| FDM | Flight Data Manager |
| FIS-B | Flight Information Service–Broadcast |
| | |
| GA | general aviation |

| | |
|---|---|
| GAO | Government Accountability Office |
| GPS | Global Positioning System |
| | |
| HITLS | human-in-the-loop simulations |
| HSI | human service interaction |
| | |
| IEEE | Institute of Electrical and Electronics Engineers |
| ISEF | integrated systems engineering framework |
| IT | information technology |
| | |
| JPDO | Joint Planning and Development Office |
| | |
| MSAW | minimum safe altitude warning |
| | |
| NAS | National Airspace System |
| | |
| NAS ISEF | National Airspace System integrated systems engineering framework |
| NextGen | Next Generation Air Transportation System |
| NIST | National Institute of Standards and Technology |
| NRC | National Research Council |
| | |
| OMB | Office of Management and Budget |
| | |
| PBN | performance-based navigation |
| Pre-RFP | pre-request for proposal |
| | |
| RF | radio frequency |
| RNAV | area navigation |
| RNP | required navigation performance |
| | |
| SBS | Surveillance and Broadcast Services |
| STARS/TAMR | Standard Terminal Automation Replacement System/ Terminal Automation Modernization and Replacement |
| SWIM | System Wide Information Management |
| | |
| TCAS | traffic collision avoidance system |
| TIS-B | Traffic Information Service-Broadcast |
| TSA | Transportation Security Administration |
| | |
| UAS | unmanned aircraft system |
| UX | user experience design |

APPENDIX C

VHF         very high frequency

WAAS        wide area augmentation system
WAM         Wide Area Multilateration

ZLA ARTCC   Los Angeles En-Route Air Traffic Control Center